• • • • •
BEYOND
BUILT

BEYOND BUILT

• • • • •

Bob Paris' Guide to Achieving the Ultimate Look

• • • • •

Bob Paris

WARNER BOOKS

A Time Warner Company

● ● ● ● ●

To Rod Jackson, for his love, support and

encouragement, without which this book would

never have been written. He's pushed me to

achieve my fullest potential in life.

Copyright © 1991 by Bob Paris

All rights reserved.

Warner Books, Inc., 666 Fifth Avenue, New York, NY 10103

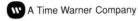 A Time Warner Company

Printed in the United States of America
First Printing: January 1991
10 9 8 7 6 5 4 3 2 1

Library of Congress Cataloging-in-Publication Data

Paris, Bob.
      Beyond built : Bob Paris' guide to achieving the ultimate look
   by Bob Paris.
          p.   cm.
      ISBN 0-446-39146-8
      1. Bodybuilding. I. Title.
   GV546.5.P37   1990
   646. 7'5—cc20   89-70571
                                                             CIP

Book Design: H. Roberts

Cover Design: Anne Twomey

Cover Photo: Mike Neveux

ACKNOWLEDGMENTS

• • • • •

The production of this book has been very much a labor of love. I love weight training and the richness it's added to my life. I grew up with body-building, so to speak. I am thankful to the sport and its pioneers for the trail that's been blazed.

I owe much gratitude to several people for their contribution to this work. Without Warner Books' senior editor Rick Horgan's enthusiasm for the project, *Beyond Built* might never have been published.

Thanks also to *MuscleMag International's* publisher, Robert Kennedy, for his help. It was Robert who first introduced me to Rick because he believed strongly that my training philosophies had to be shared.

Appreciation also to Joe and Ben Weider, two of the Trailblazers. Joe Weider has consistently supported the sport and promoted it in his publications; Ben Weider has helped also in his role as president of the International Federation of Bodybuilders (IFBB). For the past thirty-five years, he's battled to make body-building an official Olympic sport.

Great thanks to my good friend, photographer Art Zeller, who is responsible for many of the photographs contained in this book. His work has given life to each page.

Thanks also to Mike Neveux for his photo contributions. In recording body-building on film, both Art and Mike have proven themselves true artists.

CONTENTS

• • • • •

1

IN PURSUIT
OF
THE DREAM

December 14, 1959, was a fairly typical day in southern Indiana—one that found most people busying themselves in preparation for Christmas, just eleven days away. The snow and ice hadn't yet put in their appearance, but the woman being wheeled into the hospital maternity ward was wrapped in her best checkered wool coat, steam pushing in short, rapid bursts from her mouth. Less than an hour later, the doctor raised into the air the bellowing infant named Robert Clark Paris.

My first childhood memories were of the outdoors. At age four I kept my imaginary horse hitched to a tree in the woods behind my grandfather's house. I visited him daily—in full cowboy regalia. Two pistols, a hat and boots; the whole bit. He was quite an animal, that imaginary horse of mine. As hard as I tried to hold on to him, one day he just ran away. But my love for the outdoors did not.

It would provide me with an escape when the world just didn't seem to click. The need for escape came often. Our house just didn't seem to match those perfect ones I saw on TV. It would be years before I realized that *no one's* did. Perfection was just an illusion created by the turn of the television dial.

I grew up during the television era. TV brought us "Gomer Pyle—USMC," "The Carol Burnett Show," and "The Beverly Hillbillies." But it also brought us the Martin Luther King, Jr., assassination, the Watts riots, and the Vietnam War.

At home war raged between two people who years before had declared love for each other but had since walked down very different roads. My parents' antagonisms would end in divorce, remarriage to each other, and then later divorce again. I stayed in the woods a lot.

I didn't grow up in an athletic household. I guess the feeling was that energy spent on athletics could be put to better use doing "real work." Hence, being athletic, while not directly discouraged, was not encouraged either.

I can remember only one example of a sport being enthusiastically encouraged. My father loved golf. It was his passion. Everyone needs a passion, but golf wasn't mine. Dad put a golf club in my hands at eight years old and I quickly learned that the way to gain his approval was to play along.

For years during summer breaks I took golf lessons every week. A squat, grouchy man named Drex gave us lessons while chomping on a two-inch cigar butt. He was a local pro who helped make me proficient enough to at least impress Dad, who had dreams of my joining "the tour."

Oh yes, I once hit a hole in one—got a trophy and everything. My mother even witnessed it. But it just wasn't my passion. Art was my passion. I would sculpt, paint and draw. In completing one sketch, I experienced the tingles one thousand holes in one could never give me.

During my school years my art was displayed in various places, and for a long time I thought I wanted to be an architect when I grew up. In fact, most of my career desires have revolved somehow around the arts. Architecture, painting, photography, theater and eventually . . . body-building. As a boy, though, I would spend hours on end drawing house plans and pretend-blueprints.

At ten years old, I lived in the small town of Nashville, Indiana. In memory, this place still seems idyllic. Our house stood in front of a dense forest and down at the bottom of the hill was an art gallery. In it were local artists' paintings that would absorb my imagination for hours on end. Nashville was an artist's haven, and I romanticized the idea of becoming part of the "scene," displaying my paintings for all to see.

My family moved around quite a bit. It seemed like we never stayed anywhere longer than a couple of years. When I was eleven we moved back to the town where I was born, Columbus, Indiana. Columbus was a small, picturesque, midwestern farm town of about 25,000 people. Its great claim to fame was that a major industrialist who lived there had decided to hire world-famous architects to design public buildings such as the town library, schools, churches, etc. I was in heaven. I mean, here

I was living in an Indiana farm town that actually had a Henry Moore sculpture standing in front of a library designed by I. M. Pei.

When we moved to Columbus, I discovered the Boy Scouts of America. I found a troop that was extraordinarily active. It became the perfect outlet for my love of the outdoors and helped teach me community responsibility. My troop went on high-adventure back-packing, canoeing and bicycling trips all over the country, giving me valuable experience I never would have gained otherwise.

As I grew older I experienced the physical challenges that hiking twenty-five miles or cycling one hundred miles in a day could provide. The feeling of accomplishment was exhilarating. Soon I began to search for a way to combine my two loves—artistic creation and physical activity. It wasn't until I was sixteen years old that a possibility presented itself.

It's been said that in life you don't choose a path, the path chooses you. If this is so—and I've seen strong evidence to back it up—then indeed I was chosen by body-building. The first few years I trained I had no idea of my selection. I was standing in the woods surrounded by a few trees with only the vague sense that beyond me stretched an entire forest.

My image of the sport of body-building was almost nonexistent. In Columbus there weren't any gyms or health clubs. As a kid I remember seeing some body-building magazines on the newsstand. But they were cheap-looking publications that never showed the athletes inside to good effect. I'd never seen a Steve Reeves' movie, and Arnold Schwarzenegger was still years away from the screen. Many coaches were still telling their athletes that weight training would make them muscle-bound and slow.

I had a strong desire to play football. I'd tried to play football before, without great success. In the seventh grade I played on a Little League football team. The day before the second game of the season I was climbing a tree and fell about twenty feet to the ground, injuring my left forearm. I didn't tell anyone because I wanted to play ball the next day. During the game I made a tackle and heard a snap. My left arm went numb. When I went to the emergency room it was discovered that the arm was broken. I spent two months with a cast.

The next year I was going to play on the junior high team. The first day of practice we were doing tackling drills. I was running the ball and the kid playing defense hit me just as I planted my left leg. My body twisted while my foot remained firmly in place. I heard a crunch, looked down, and saw that my foot was facing the wrong direction. The assistant coach told me, "It's just a sprain . . . jog back to the school" (about a quarter of a mile away). He was apparently making a point about "manhood." I managed to get up, fall down, then crawl, dragging my left leg behind me. A kid named Jeff finally came and helped me get back to the school, where an ambulance was called to take me to the hospital.

After X rays, my doctor discovered that I had a severe spiral break that cut into the growth center of the bone. He said that if I'd tried to take even one more step I could have lost my leg. This time the cast was on for five months.

In the ninth grade a different type of accident dashed my football hopes. My Boy Scout troop was cleaning out horse stalls on our scoutmaster's father-in-law's farm one Saturday. During a break for lunch a herd of unbroken horses came up to us in the field. I decided it would be cool to ride an unbroken horse bareback and was up on this huge animal before I even thought about it. He took off at a gallop, reared up and threw me over his head. I reached out with my right arm to break the fall, and as I landed there was that familiar cracking noise. Once again, I was rushed to the emergency room, where they now knew me on sight. The doctor set the compound fracture in my right arm and put me in a cast for the next three months.

As a sophomore I finally achieved some success on the gridiron. At least, I didn't break any bones. I made it through the season, but I wanted to be bigger, faster and stronger. At this point I weighed 170 pounds.

I was athletic from all my cycling, backpacking and running, but I had no real muscle size. Since I lived in a farming community, my grandfather suggested I build myself up by working in the fields baling hay. This, of course, was about as appealing as drinking a quart of castor oil.

As it happened, I was on a menial errand at my high school gymnasium one day when quite by accident I went into the weight training room looking for some object I couldn't find. I took the chance that it might be there—behind that door. The moment I touched the knob and pushed myself inside I felt as if my pockets were loaded with magnets, urging me to find some connection inside that dark, strange-smelling room. When I turned on the lights, I felt like I'd just turned a corner in some foreign city where no one speaks your language. There, spelled out on a wall, was the answer to a question that had been bothering me for days. And it was written in *English:* NO PAIN—NO GAIN.

Occupying the center of the room was an old Universal multistation machine with selectorized weights. I began to play around at the various exercises, not really knowing what I was doing, and it felt absolutely familiar and right. I felt my muscles contract and work in a way no other sport had affected them. I did hundreds of reps of bench presses, leg presses, pulldowns and curls.

The next morning I woke up and thought I was paralyzed. Intense pain raced through my arms and legs. I couldn't reach up to comb my hair or brush my teeth. My body stayed at that pain level for about a week, and over the next week I slowly got mobility back in my limbs.

When I returned to normal I went back to the weight room. I knew I'd found something that felt very right. During the next few weeks I began testing my strength in the various exercises. Thinking back on it now, I realize I had a natural feel for the exercises. I felt contractions in my muscles during every workout. If I didn't get the right feel, I'd experiment with the exercise until I found it. This was an instinct that I would hone and perfect in the years ahead.

When I began training I became aware of my body structure for the first time. The soreness enabled me to feel every muscle fiber and insertion throughout my whole body. I began looking in the mirror with a critical eye. I realized that I'd always been slightly embarrassed by my body. It felt strangely shaped. I had huge chunky legs, a flat chest and skinny arms.

I kept my workouts consistent and watched as over the months muscles began popping out all over. My strength levels also dramatically increased. During my first workouts I was barely able to do 150 pounds on the Universal machine bench press. After several workouts, with my mind and body learning the grooves of the exercises, I was using 220 pounds for repetitions. I'm sure I would have increased even more, but 220 was the limit of the weight stack, so once that level was reached I just kept doing more and more reps. I was feeling very stifled by the limited amount of equipment that was available. I had to be extremely creative with my workouts and began developing routines that would add variety to the training.

It had been halfway into the second semester of my sophomore year that I first discovered the school weight room. I trained consistently until the end of the school year. During that time my body weight increased about ten pounds. When summer vacation arrived I was concerned that the school would be closed and that I wouldn't have access to the gym. When our football coach agreed to open the room during limited hours every other day, I was in heaven. The minute the doors opened, I'd be there, ready for my first set. I would sink myself into deep concentration and train until closing two hours later. I was so focused that the two hours seemed like five minutes. A few other athletes would come to train also, but it always was different for me. They seemed to view the workout as partly social, talking and laughing during sets. I was the "weirdo" who didn't say a word and moved from one exercise to the next like a machine.

During that summer my body experienced its first dramatic change. I went from 180 pounds to 200 pounds and my strength shot up. I no longer had a flat chest and my arms weren't skinny. My bulky legs were taking shape and my back was getting a V-taper. My abdominals were a problem, though. I had no idea what constituted good nutrition. I figured I needed to eat meat to gain muscle, so I did. I ate a whole bunch of steak and hamburger. Unfortunately, potato chips, cookies and milk shakes were my other dietary staples. I had a lot to learn.

That same summer my Boy Scout troop was scheduled to hike three miles to a wooded camp in our area—Camp Louis Ernest. I decided that I wasn't going to miss any workouts while at camp, so I carried a home barbell set I'd purchased back into the woods with me. At the time it seemed like the longest walk ever. You never realize how heavy 100 pounds is until you walk three miles up and down hills with it on your back! I was determined, to say the least.

In body-building, people usually find camaraderie and companionship or solitude and peace. I found the latter. Training in the woods just as the sun was coming up was amazingly peaceful. I couldn't imagine a greater feeling or greater reward for carrying my weights through the hills. The reward felt even greater when I realized that this was something I'd *earned*.

My junior year I showed up for the first football practice with a much stronger and larger body, and it paid off. Oh, I still wasn't a great football player, but my performance level increased dramatically, and I was extraordinarily disciplined. At home my parents were completing their divorce, and I really believe that the solitude and goals I found in exercising helped me keep my sanity.

Even though I was finding a direction with exercise, in school I lacked true concentration. I'd always been a good student, but much of what we studied seemed unnecessary. I liked the teachers who taught me how to learn and hated the ones who shoved stale, lifeless old lectures down my throat. More than anything, I wanted to get out in the world and learn everything firsthand. For me the greatest education was experience. I kept my eyes and ears open and soaked up all the "real" knowledge I could handle.

Throughout the rest of high school I continued my training. Sometimes it was sporadic. At times I would skip a couple of weeks or a month, but the gym was always there, ready for me to return and take up where I'd left off.

I played football again my senior year, but my heart wasn't really in it. I'd discovered the sport of body-building. It first happened when I picked up an issue of *Rolling Stone* and saw a feature article on Arnold Schwarzenegger. Instantly, he became my role model. A few weeks later I found an issue of *Muscle Builder* (now *Muscle and Fitness*) on the newsstand and my heart raced with the excitement of finding a new way to look at my training. Up to this point I'd seen my workouts as something done to improve performance for another sport. But here was a sport all its own dedicated to weight training. I began to buy all the body-building magazines each month. I would pester the woman at the newsstand for days until a new edition of *Muscle Builder* would arrive. I had a problem, though. I was reading about all the routines of the champions and getting psyched to try them out, but my gym wasn't set up for it. I'd definitely outgrown it, and longed for a fully equipped gym.

After graduation I decided to go to college. But after one semester I knew I needed to get out into the world. I understood that formal education was important, but it would have to come at a later point.

One of the positive contributions college made to my life was teaching me what it was like to train in a real gym. The first day I arrived at Indiana State I went to the basketball gymnasium to find a place to train. I was expecting something similar to high school and was thrilled when I walked into the basement and found enclosed behind an indoor track and chain-link fence what seemed like every body-building "toy" imaginable. There were olympic bars and dumbbells, benches and squat racks. Over the next couple of months I began to meet people who shared my interest in the sport. We talked about reps, sets, nutrition and what competition must be like. I was experimenting with all the training philosophies I'd been reading about in the magazines. The seeds were planted. I was definitely going to compete.

I felt once again as if there were magnets in my pockets. It was 1979 and I had been reading about Southern California the past couple of years in the body-building magazines. Also, I'd been very active in plays and theater in high school and wanted to be an actor. Acting was a way for me to get beyond just me and gave me the freedom to be different and creative with an excuse. California, therefore, seemed like the most logical destination.

When I arrived I immediately threw myself into body-building. I worked jobs that would give me the time to train and I began to ask question after question about body-building, always thirsting for new knowledge of the sport. I began a process of experimenting with different training techniques and drawing knowledge from as many different sources as possible, including olympic and power lifters at the first California gym where I worked. I kept what my gut told me was right and discarded the rest.

I had made a move that I would only recommend to someone with a strong sense of adventure and spontaneity. I was living for my training and making the remainder of my life fit around it. It was not the most stable or pragmatic approach to success, but I felt like someone who'd just escaped from an oppressive country and had arrived in a "free" land. I could not concern myself with what I didn't have, only build upon what I did.

What I did have was heart and determination, the drive to succeed. I was going to take what genetic talent I had and create a success story. If I had to live in my car for a while to accomplish that, then so be it. I would just have that many more colorful memories to look back on later. All I could see at the moment was the future.

I believe that everything in life happens for a reason. I *had* to struggle financially to keep from competing before I was ready. I was not ready yet. I had just barely begun proper training in a halfway decently equipped gym. I didn't even know my body yet. I was a beginner, an apprentice, and I needed to respect that level. I needed to acknowledge the level I was on before I could move on to the next. Looking at it realistically, I had only been training for three years, and two of those years had been spent using an old, rusty Universal machine and a plastic-coated, 100-pound home barbell set.

The lesson I needed to learn was patience. I saw my body-building from a "quantum leap" perspective. I knew I was capable of the hard work that would yield gains in steady increments, so I mentally projected myself into the future. I knew the end result. I would fill in the gaps as I went along.

My goals became clear: only compete in the most prestigious shows; win the Mr. Los Angeles, then the Mr. America and the Mr. Universe.

I remember a time that I told someone about part of that goal. I had been in California for about six months and was working and training at a gym that attracted competitive body-builders. During a conversation I told one of the guys that I would be a Mr. America in five years. I wasn't just stroking my ego, I was speaking matter-of-factly. I knew in my heart it was true.

This guy started laughing so hard that I thought he was going to hurt himself. Then he started giving me a lecture about how that wasn't possible. He thought that with some luck I could maybe place somewhere around fifth in my weight class. I decided at that point to keep my goals to myself and not expose them to small-minded people who couldn't see beyond their noses. He was right about one thing, though: I didn't win the Mr. America in five years. I won it in three. That, I learned, was the power of dreams and hard work.

I saw the world from an artist's point of view. When I looked at people I saw portraits. When I looked at scenery I thought of how I

would paint, draw or photograph it. So naturally, I saw body-building as an artistic pursuit. I read how Frank Zane thought of the weights as hammers and chisels and his body as sculpture, and I agreed completely. I still do.

During the first two years I was in California I really began to embrace the idea of body-building as a combination of sport and art. I had body parts that grew much faster than others. My structure dictated that my legs were the fastest-growing part of my physique. My chest development tended to lag behind. I started looking with a critical eye at all my different body parts to determine which areas needed the most attention.

I'd alter my workouts accordingly to fit this overall design. I kept a daily journal where workouts and food intake were recorded in detail. I looked to body-building to help me transcend the normal. If others saw me as strange for my career choice, I saw it as taking my body, mind and spirit to a higher place, and that suited me just fine.

One of the unfortunate aspects of my early years in California was that I lost interest in the outdoors. I was so focused on my goals that for three or four years I forgot what sitting on a hilltop listening to the wind sing truly meant. I had a certain emptiness that would sometimes make me sad. Have you ever dropped a penny into a well and made a wish? You finally hear the coin hit and the sound of the little ripples slowly making their way up the sides of the well. To me that is a very lonely sound and it gives me a hollow feeling. That is the feeling I had deep inside. It was at this point that I began to realize that my life needed balancing.

In the fall of 1980 I entered my first show. I had been in California for just over a year and had developed, in my mind's eye, a picture of my ideal physique. During the time between leaving Indiana and competing in my first show, I had come across many different attitudes toward the sport. Most emphasized building as much muscle as possible, everywhere possible. Many were influenced by the "How much can you bench?" mentality. I considered both of these viewpoints dead-end streets. The first led to creating an ugly, monstrous physique and the second made you a slave to your own ego. I wanted to get past those traps that I saw many body-builders fall into. So in the months leading up to my first contest I trained to sculpt my physique; I forgot about the poundages I was able to lift and began focusing totally on the feel of the muscle and the intensity of each set.

Robby Robinson was, then and now, one of my body-building heroes. When I first started buying the magazines, Robby was "the Black Prince" and someone whose physical development I wanted to emulate. I was inspired by the great battle he'd given Frank Zane in the 1978 and 1979 Mr. Olympia contests.

In 1980, Robby promoted the Robby Robinson Classic in Los

Angeles. Since Robby was one of my heroes, I wanted to make my amateur debut in his show. I trained with incredible intensity and dieted seriously for the first time. I had spent much of the year learning as much as I could about nutrition. But I still had a long way to go. I was getting most of my input from athletes who believed in *bulking up* forty or fifty pounds above contest weight and then using extreme dieting techniques to get *cut up* for competition.

I would learn that this is a self-destructive cycle and that once it has started it's very difficult to break out of. I discovered that this up-and-down cycle was in reality not only bad for my health but also a type of eating disorder. Later, I discovered the value of balancing my nutrition on a year-round basis.

But in 1980 I knew only *bulking up* and *cutting down.* I competed in the Robby Robinson Classic at 180 pounds. I liked what I saw, but the extreme diet I'd been on had caused me to lose muscle as well as fat. I was pretty nervous on stage. I'd put together a posing routine with the help of a body-builder who was considered a good poser. Even though the routine was thoroughly rehearsed I was shaking during the performance. I placed a very close second.

I went back to the gym and began planning for my next show. I analyzed photos from the last contest and reviewed my journals. I was looking for weaknesses to improve upon. I altered routines to develop lagging body parts and worked to create greater muscle size and symmetry. I set my sights on the Mr. Los Angeles in the spring of 1981. The Mr. Los Angeles is the most prestigious local contest in the world. It attracts a higher level of competition than any state contest (except maybe the Mr. California) and is regarded as a springboard to the national level. During the months between the Robby Robinson Classic and the Mr. Los Angeles, I made dramatic improvements in my overall shape and entered the show at 190 pounds.

Standing onstage at the Mr. L.A., I realized that all my dreams were coming true. Here I was, less than two years after leaving Indiana, competing at this level.

I was not only competing, I was going to *win* and I had stuck to my ideals. I also realized that I wasn't just here because of some sort of freaky genetics. I had made rapid progress because I was dedicated to learning how to perfect my individual potential.

To keep the dream alive I had to continue to grow—mentally, physically and emotionally. Up to this point, I'd been living in Orange County—sort of the suburbs of L.A. I had purposely decided not to jump into the middle of the body-building world of Santa Monica and Venice until I was strong and mature enough to not take it too seriously. I had heard countless stories about novice body-builders filled with big dreams coming from all over the world, throwing their lives completely into "the scene," only to get chewed up and spit out. So I kept myself on the fringe, learning the ropes and establishing a reputation as a body-builder with "pro" potential.

I viewed my body-building progress as a chess game—a game that would require planning and intelligence to win. I was developing a strategy that would take me to the top of the sport.

By 1982, the chess board was set. All the pieces had fallen into

Competing with Robby Robinson.

position for an assault on professional status. Two important moves took place that year, tilting the game in my favor: World Gym and Weider.

World Gym had a reputation as a quiet, serious place. The place where Arnold and Zane trained. I had driven by many times but had always felt too intimidated to go inside. Now I was not only going inside, I was going to train there. Of the two major Santa Monica–Venice gyms, World Gym, I knew instinctively, would better suit my personality and needs. The day I walked up the stairs, I knew I'd found a new home for my training. The gym had a quiet energy that literally bounced off the walls. There was no music, only the sound of weights moving and people getting down to the work at hand.

I stood in the doorway about thirty seconds before the owner, Joe Gold, descended on me and asked in a no-nonsense, gruff voice, "Yes, may I help you?" I would learn it was his way of intimidating the riffraff and protecting his sacred ground and the people inside. In time, I would be one of those on the "inside," but I certainly didn't get there immediately. I was going to have to prove myself, and I was glad of that.

In this place the energy and history of those who had come before me motivated me to quantum-leap improvements. The equipment was incredible. Not fancy, but made by hands that knew what training was all about. The dumbbells were all tight, no one ever dropped them (for fear of being banished from the place) and they were racked in order.

The first contest I prepared for at World was the 1982 Mr. America in New York (the "Mr. America" title was changed to "N.P.C. National Championships" in 1983). This was the year Lee Haney began his march through the big leagues. I placed third and knew deep in my heart that the next year the title would be mine.

About a week after the show, Rick Wayne phoned the gym and said that Joe Weider wanted him to interview me for *Muscle and Fitness*. I accepted and we met the next week at the gym. Rick would turn out to be one of my biggest supporters in the body-building media. His initial articles focused a huge amount of attention on my career before I'd even won a national competition.

Around this time, I also met Joe Weider and began developing an up-and-down but always enduring business relationship and friendship. A lot of people in body-building condemn Joe for any number of reasons, but he's earned my respect because of his commitment and love for the sport.

Over the next year I began working with a number of talented people in the body-building media, including photographic talents Mike Neveux, John Balik and Art Zeller.

In the gym, I got down to serious business. I found a drive inside that spurred my body to changes I never thought I could make. The commitment paid off when I won the 1983 American Nationals and then three weeks later amateur body-building's most prestigious title, the IFBB Mr. Universe.

Checkmate.

After winning the America and Universe, my calendar began filling up with guest-posing spots in every corner of the world. I had already been doing seminars in the States for about a year, but now I was traveling internationally every month and guest-posing almost every weekend. I began working with different charity organizations—the American Diabetes Association, the American A.I.D.S. Foundation, etc.—trying to give back some of my good fortune to others. Over the next two years I trained very hard to make the kind of improvement needed to be a successful pro. In my pro debut, at the 1984 Mr. Olympia, I placed seventh. I had never placed lower than third in any contest, so it was a bit of a shock, but I was happy with the improvements and the showing I'd made. I wanted to be Mr. Olympia, but it had to be on my terms and according to the standards I'd set for how I wanted my body to look.

In 1985 the story was similar. I was very much in demand for guest appearances; my magazine covers were best-sellers; my physique was being hailed as among the most complete and symmetrical in the world. But at the Mr. Olympia I placed ninth. It was time for a change. Most people thought I was just coming into my own, but I began to feel that I'd accomplished all that I could in the sport. Other goals had to be pursued.

I had moved to California with two distinct goals in mind. The first was to be a successful body-builder. The second was to be an actor. I wanted to be a real actor. While in high school I'd been a member of the International Thespian Society, and was really fortunate to have been influenced by a good drama department and a talented director, who led our school productions.

When I got to California my body-building goals headed my priority list. I put my theater goals on hold, but I knew they'd always be there. Acting was as much in my blood as body-building.

Shortly after the 1985 Mr. Olympia, I began looking for an acting school. I didn't want to be just another musclehead who did stereotypical bit parts. I wanted to learn and perfect acting skills the same way I'd prepared myself as a body-builder. So I auditioned at one of the top conservatories in Los Angeles and was accepted to begin full-time study from the ground up. It was when I was accepted to this school that I retired from competitive body-building. At the time I said my retirement was forever, and I believed it. For nearly two years I threw myself into the theater and the perfection of the acting craft. I dramatically reduced my body weight to a "normal" size to be able to play a variety of classic roles. I was studying on a full-time basis, taking hours of class each day and doing an equal amount of homework each night. I was completely, intensely involved. I was moving from beginning to advanced levels at a rapid pace, partly due to my goal-setting skills and the work ethic I'd learned as an athlete.

Just as I didn't compete as an athlete until I was ready, I purposely decided to not pursue any theater work until I'd earned the right to present my talent.

One of the networks wanted me to do a soap opera. I had prospective scripts coming in from all over the world. But I'd done some TV work a few years earlier while still body-building and it felt like going on a competition stage without knowing how to pose. I was unprepared. I decided to never put myself in that position again. So I didn't go to any auditions or pursue work—I studied and grew.

As my two-year conservatory program came to a close, I was preoccupied with the decision of whether to audition for a repertory company, pursue a film career or continue studying. The day after my program finally ended, I drove out to the desert. As I'd done in the past, I sat on my favorite rock, asking myself, "Where do I go from here?" It was then that I realized I was at a major crossroads in my life. I'd been successful at my sport and now I was successfully learning a new craft. The one thing I hadn't done was give myself a chance to find out if I could take body-building even further. I'd left the sport partly out of frustration and partly because I thought I'd gone as far as I could.

But here I was sitting in the desert and all that kept popping into my head was "You didn't give yourself a chance." I wondered how this could be happening. I'd just invested two tough years in beginning to learn another skill after keeping it on the back burner for five years. I walked back to the car, got in and drove home.

All the way home I kept thinking about how much further I could have pushed myself as an athlete. When I got home, I went to bed and had an intense, vivid dream. I dreamed of being on stage at the Mr.

Olympia. For four nights in a row I had this same dream. During the day, I thought about the power of regret. I was now twenty-seven years old and I realized that if I proceeded any further away from body-building, I would never go back to it. I decided that I didn't want to be sixty years old and regret not giving myself one more chance while I was still a young man. For the past two years I'd been studying, but I didn't have a career developed yet. I hadn't walked too far away from body-building and so I decided to put my acting aspirations on hold for just a while longer. I headed to the gym. I went right back into full-bore contest training, competing again within six months. I very quickly realized that I *hadn't* completed my body-building goals. I returned to the dream that inspired a sixteen-year-old boy to carry 100 pounds of weight three miles through the woods just so he wouldn't miss a workout. I was once more in love with the sport and making more progress than ever.

Recently I got married and moved to a small town in Washington state. It's surrounded by mountains and woods and is the perfect environment to pursue the goals that are spinning around inside my head, becoming clearer day by day.

2

. . . . .

STARTING

OUT

. . . . .

Apercentage of people reading
this book are newcomers to body-building. This chapter is for you. It's
dedicated to those of you who are just beginning your weight training
and who may be intimidated, not only by the gym, but also by what
society has drilled into your head about body-building. "Don't work out
or you'll become muscle-bound," you may have been told, or if you're a
woman, "Muscles are a man's domain." That's just not true. Just turn
on the TV, go to the movies or flip through any magazine. Pick out your
favorite body. Pick the one you would like yours to look like. There's a
99 percent chance that that person trains. Today's best bodies are
trained bodies, and with the fitness boom forging ahead it becomes
more true day by day.

Using the techniques in this book you'll learn how to sculpt your
body whether you're training for shape and tone or to be a competitive
body-builder. Those of you who aren't interested in developing a
competitive physique, but who worry that if you work out you'll build one
no matter what you do, please note: The women and men who are on

stage competing have spent *years* training and dieting to achieve their competitive status. Sprouting huge muscles by doing a recreational weight workout is as unlikely as being able to create a new computer program simply by sitting down at the keyboard.

For those of you who've never been "athletic," this is the perfect opportunity to develop the physical aspect of your nature. The beauty of fitness training is that you compete against no one but yourself. You decide your own level and intensity. You set your own pace and develop your own challenges.

Throughout this book I have tried to be as nongender-specific as possible. The road one takes toward mastering weight training is the same whether you're a woman or a man. Our physiologies and skeletal structures are very much the same.

I fully believe that whether you're a man or a woman, weight training can play a vital role in perfecting your individual potential. Properly used, training can be a tool to get in touch with how your body works and what works best for your body. So let's begin at square one.

Home or gym training—which is best? You're probably going to learn faster by joining a gym. Personalized instruction is ideal, but you should always question the trainer. Don't just take advice from anyone. At the very least you can learn some basics from other gym members. The plus side of training at a commercial gym is that you have access to a large variety of heavy-duty equipment that most people could never afford to put in their own homes, even if they had the room.

On the other hand, the beauty of home training is that you can work out at any time you wish. You're not dependent on an establishment that has set business hours.

Newcomers to body-building should work out three times a week. Depending on your energy levels, available time and natural enthusiasm, these workouts will normally take about an hour to complete. Make sure that you have a rest day between each workout. The majority of beginners seem to train on Mondays, Wednesdays and Fridays, which leaves the weekend free for family or other pursuits, but there are other workable combinations that you can tailor to your own individual needs, family and work obligations—for example, Tuesdays, Thursdays and Saturdays.

My own choice, although I vary my frequency patterns in keeping with my philosophy of maintaining variety in training, is usually to follow a three-days-on, one-day-off schedule. I divide my routine into three sections, performing a workout three days in a row. The fourth day is a rest day. After that, the whole process is started again. Here's how I divide my body parts for this particular frequency:

Day 1
Chest
Shoulders
Triceps
Abs

Day 2
Front thigh
Hamstrings
Calves
Lower back

Day 3
Back
Biceps
Forearms

Day 4
Rest

If you're a newcomer to body-building, though, you should stick to the three-times-a-week pattern. If you try to cram more workouts into your training week, you'll overstress the muscles.

Sweats and tennis shoes are ideal workout wear. In cold weather you'll want to put on layers of T-shirts and sweat tops. You'll still have the looseness needed to perform the selected exercises, but the air trapped between the various layers will keep your muscles warm. Plus, if the temperature rises, or you start to become overheated, you can peel off some of your clothing to maintain your comfort level.

There are a lot of different theories about how beginning body-building should get started. Obviously, there wouldn't be so many books, glossy magazines, courses and instructional classes if there weren't room for a lot of discussion.

So needless to say, I have my own theory. It didn't come to me in a dream. It has resulted from years of experience. Never mind what others tell you. For better or for worse you are reading *my* book at this moment in time. You have displayed at least a degree of confidence in what I have to say. Follow my beginner's program here. It's been carefully designed to get you to make the most of your individual potential.

I want you to make a silent promise to yourself, a commitment to stay with body-building for six weeks. Many people give up after three or four workouts, but I believe if they could have stuck it out for six weeks, the benefits would have been obvious . . . and they would never have quit. So make a contract with yourself now . . . to train for six weeks—minimum.

During these six weeks, don't look for miraculous changes in your physique. Look for the small changes that will take place and realize that similar changes will take place each month that you continue to train. Twelve months in a row of incremental progress will add up to big changes at the end of the year. For example, if during those six weeks you learn how to feel your muscles contract and you increase your bench-press strength by twenty pounds, and your pants become slightly baggier in the waist, you know you're on your way.

Building a body is like building a house. You need to start by laying a strong base. You build from the foundation up. It's no good trying to run before you can walk.

The most fundamental thing about progressive resistance training (body-building) is that you exercise *all* the muscles of the body. Even if you possess "good legs," "wide shoulders" or some other highly developed feature, you should exercise every body part enthusiastically. You may not need added size in some areas, but you'll still have to train every body part to maintain evenly balanced muscle quality and tone.

Beginners may be only vaguely familiar with the terms *sets* and *reps.* Both are vital to the workout. A *rep*, or repetition, is one count of an exercise. In other words, if you press up a weight from your shoulders to the arms-straight position overhead, and lower it again, that is known as a rep. Do it twice, two reps, three times is three reps . . . got it?

A *set* is a series of reps that you perform with very little, if any, pause. Typically, a set consists of eight or twelve reps, but there are occasions when considerably less or many more are used. At the conclusion of a set you replace the weight, usually on the floor or racks (as in the case of bench presses and squats, for example).

Newcomers to body-building can train the whole body in one workout, although as time goes on you will be adding exercises (and sets); and consequently, as your workout gets longer, you'll find that it's next to impossible to do justice to every body part. If you don't run out of gas (energy) you'll run out of time. As this stage approaches you'll find it convenient to cut your workout in two, performing the first half one day and the second half the next day. Ultimately, this leads to a weekly workout schedule composed of four, five or even six training sessions.

One of the most common sights at any gym is young trainers working out using terrible exercise style. Their arms are wobbling during bench presses. They lean too far forward, their heads down, during squats. Heavy weights are bounced mercilessly off the chest. They lean back too far during standing presses and curls. Pulleys are jerked; leg extensions are bounced; rows are hoisted and incline presses are heaved. . . . Little wonder there are injuries.

But that's not the only reason why beginners should avoid poor exercise style. Sloppy training doesn't fully work the muscles. Precise, full-extension, relatively slow movements are what work the muscles. The beginner should be concerned only with *feeling* the exercise, not with hoisting up heavier and heavier weights. Your repetitions should be

nonballistic. No bouncing or swinging. Make the muscles do the work in a steady up-down rhythm. The weight should be raised and lowered at the same speed. Your reps should be done almost in slow motion, *finding* the fibers along the way. Think of pouring molasses from a jar on a winter's day and you'll realize what I'm trying to get across. Body-building repetitions are all about stretching and contracting the fibers, not straining to lift all the  weight you can. For this reason I say with all seriousness: Before you start your workout, *hang your ego at the gym door!*

Beginners must use the rehearsal method. Learn all about your body; touch it, feel the various parts of your body. Observe yourself in the mirror. Know your muscles inside and out. You need to develop the mind-muscle link. Do your homework. Learn as much about your body as possible. Body-building is a craft. You start as an apprentice and eventually, if you stick with it, progress all the way to mastery. As an apprentice you should follow the *rules* of the game. It's on the basis of these rules that you will develop the self-knowledge and instinct to advance to the next level. When you reach that level you will have earned the right to change the rules, or even to invent a few principles of your own.

Your first duty in the gym is to warm up. Get your blood flowing, your heart pumping, with five or ten minutes on a stationary bike, or by simply running in place, doing aerobic dancing or jumping rope for a few minutes at a very moderate pace. Stretching, too, is very important. At the beginning of a workout the muscles are like cold rubber bands...we need to loosen them with five to ten minutes of warming and stretching.

The repetition count most often recommended for weight training is eight to twelve, but beginners should perform fifteen to twenty reps during their early workouts, because they need to find the correct "groove" for each exercise. They need to learn to control and balance the weight, build the neuromuscular nerve pathways, and above all "find" the right muscle contraction. (More on this later.) All this is done by rehearsal. The higher reps will open up the pathways quicker, build control and carve in the grooves. Use very light weights to start with; think about each and every repetition. Stretch out each one to the maximum extension and contraction.

Your workout routine should be designed to develop all parts equally to create a balanced physique. However, you'll have no idea at first how quickly each body part will grow. Some people find that their chest and back increase quickly in size, while their legs are slow to respond. Others find that their arms grow faster than all the other body parts. It's a matter of personal makeup. One thing's pretty certain: everyone has body-part areas that respond better than others. This is the time for self-observation. Get as much feedback from the mirror as possible and use what you see to analyze your training and change your routine from workout to workout. It's a good idea to keep a training journal, recording every exercise, set and repetition count. It becomes your personal computer, your information control. I will illustrate in a later chapter how to lay out your journal. It's not at all difficult, and with the information you record you'll find that body-building does become, ultimately, something of a science.

When you're starting out, don't copy the routines of the superstars of body-building. Remember, they all started with a foundation. You have to begin at the beginning by learning to perfect the rep. If you look at body-building as being like a cellular structure, then the smallest portion of the workout becomes the rep. Endeavor to make each rep perfect.

Ultimately, you'll perfect the set, then the exercise and, finally, the entire workout.

One mistake beginners make is that they assume that more is actually better. Nothing could be further from the truth. When you engage in mammoth training sessions you require a long time to recover (up to a week). Advanced athletes learn to recover relatively quickly, but as a beginner your body has not yet learned to recover efficiently from strenuous weight training. Until this happens workouts will have to be abbreviated and brisk to avoid overtraining, which can easily occur at any time. The symptoms are tiredness, flat-looking muscles, oversoreness and a general lack of interest in training. On the other hand, you should learn to differentiate between genuine, hard-core fatigue and mere laziness. You must be honest with yourself and listen to your body.

The question of how long to rest between sets often confuses people. There is no simple answer, but as a general guideline you should wait until your breathing pattern has pretty much returned to normal. You'll find that more rest is required to catch your breath after a high-rep set of squats than a high-rep set of curls. Some individuals have a strong fitness level and are ready for the next set almost immediately, but generally, a rest of sixty to ninety seconds between sets is ideal. You don't want to make your exercise cardiovascular in nature, because if your lungs are still struggling to get air you won't be comfortable enough to do justice to your muscles.

Training is like reading a novel. Don't make excuses not to open the book. Don't flick the pages and miss the crux of the story. And remember: If you stop reading and return the book to the shelf you'll never get the chance to see how the characters develop. Keep with your body-building.

THE EXERCISES

One reason for writing this book is to get beginners, and even some nonbeginners, to perform the exercises correctly. A perfect physique can be built with perfect exercise form. It's easy to be overanxious in the sport. We all want success yesterday. But we have to learn to slow down. Use body-building as a tool to get to know your body better. Don't fall into the beginner's trap of trying to see how much weight you can lift. I can't count the times I've watched beginners "try their strength" only to lose control and have the whole weight come crashing down. The typical scenario—two guys talking: "Can you lift it?" "Nah! Can *you*?" "Sure, watch this!" The bar is hoisted awkwardly to the shoulders and an attempt to push it overhead is made. One side wobbles up higher than the other; the weight discs slide off and crash to the floor. Immediately, the unbalanced side tilts and the weight discs on that side slide off. Big noise, big damage; lots of embarrassment. Has this happened to you? Make sure it doesn't. Remember: *Hang your ego at the gym door!*

It may not be vital, because muscles can be built in a dozen different ways, but I personally believe that best results come from a system that combines barbell and dumbbell movements, as well as free-weight machines, such as the crossover chest apparatus, the leg-extension unit and the various lat machines.

Are you ready for your first workout? It will take longer than usual, because you're going to follow my directions to the letter. I want you to start right—and that's why your first day's training will be a rehearsal workout. Use only the bar (twenty pounds) on most exercises, perhaps a small amount of weight on movements like rowing, squats and bench presses. Think back to what I said about building grooves and forging strong nerve pathways. Perfect your rep now and you will benefit enormously in the long run. Conversely, if you load the bar up and try your darndest to get "eight reps or die," you'll find yourself falling into the habit of using sloppy exercise style—a habit that can be extremely difficult to break.

Follow my suggested exercise form and once it becomes "second nature" you'll be able to maintain and benefit from it for as long as you continue to train. The following is your arsenal of exercises from which your workouts will be designed.

Back

Bent-over row (overall back thickness). Stand with the feet comfortably apart, bending over at the waist, knees slightly bent. The legs should take the balance of the weight, not the lower back, because there is incredible pressure on the lumbar region. Hold your head up as though looking in a mirror, flex the back and pull the barbell to the chest, finding the flex of the back. Hold it for a split second and lower the weight, reaching down to fully stretch the lats. Don't turn this exercise into a hyperextension movement by raising the torso each repetition.

Wide-grip front pulldown (lat width). Take a slightly wider-than-shoulders grip. Keep the body upright, raise the rib cage, arch the back slightly. Pull the elbows downward. As the bar approaches the sternum, "find" the contraction, pause for half a beat and almost in slow motion allow the resistance to pull your arms to the straight position. Execute this movement as much as possible by pure lat power. Endeavor to keep the arms (biceps) not involved.

Bent-Over _Row_ (start)

Bent-Over _Row_ (finish)

Wide-Grip Front Pulldown (start)

Wide-Grip Front Pulldown (finish)

One-arm dumbbell row (middle and lower lat). Place one knee on a flat exercise bench and establish a strong position by placing your other leg in a prop position. Keeping your shoulders in a natural position, extend all the way down to stretch the lat muscle fully. Use your hand as a hook to hold the dumbbell, keeping the elbow above the hand throughout the entire movement. Bring the dumbbell as high as possible to reach the maximum contraction point, but not so high as to twist the body around. Try to only contract the back muscles. If you are new to this movement you will not find complete contractions during your early workout, because the pathways have to open up and this takes time.

Hyperextensions (lower back). Probably the finest lower back exercise. Start by making yourself comfortable in the facedown position on a hyperextension bench. Place your hands as shown in the illustration and raise the torso upwards as high as possible, holding the contraction for a split second before lowering, slowly.

One-Arm Dumbbell Row (finish)

One-Arm Dumbbell Row (start)

Hyperextensions (start)

Hyperextensions (finish)

Chest

Flat bench press (overall pectorals). Lie on a flat bench in the supine (face-up) position. Raise the rib cage slightly without arching the back excessively. Shoulders must be in a natural position. Hold the bar with a comfortable wider-than-shoulders hand spacing. Lower the bar under control to just above the middle of the chest. No bouncing. Rather than pressing the bar with arm power, try and lift it by mentally contracting the pectorals. Squeeze the bar back to the arms-straight position. As the arms almost lock out, squeeze hands around the bar and "find" the pectoral contraction.

Throughout the movement the body should be kept solid—feet flat on the floor, glutes flat on the bench. Remember, we've checked our ego at the door, so there's no squirming to get the weight up. Don't mimic others who use the bench press as an ego trip to try and impress others.

Incline bench press (upper pectoral areas). The usual angle for this is forty-five degrees. Make sure that you are sitting right back into the bench. Feet should be wide apart and set solidly on the ground. Keep the elbows back throughout the lift. Don't lift hips off bench by excessive back arching. The movement then becomes identical to flat bench press. If you find yourself straining and arching to complete your reps, reduce the amount of weight on the bar.

Incline dumbbell flye (upper-outer pectorals). Start by lying back on a forty-five-degree incline bench. Place feet firmly on the ground. Hold the dumbbells above your head, arms slightly bent at all times. Lower slowly to the low-stretch position, seeking to "feel" the stretch across the chest muscles. Do not "bounce" the weights at this low position. Using exclusive pectoral contractions, squeeze the weights back together again. Picture in your mind a spring being compressed as you lower the dumbbells—and "see it" releasing as you lift up. In this way the kinetic energy for lifting the weight is building, so that you can return the dumbbells to the overhead position with more confidence.

Flat _Bench_ _Press_ (start)

Flat _Bench_ _Press_ (finish)

Incline Bench Press (start)

Incline Bench Press (finish)

Incline Dumbbell Flye (start)

Incline Dumbbell Flye (finish)

Legs

The _squat_ (overall frontal thigh).   Really, a rack is needed for safe squatting; even a workout partner is not a suitable substitute.   Secure a loaded barbell across the back of the head (where the traps meet the neck). You can place a towel around the bar if you find it particularly uncomfortable.   Place your heels on a three-quarter-inch-high block of wood.   Keep feet approximately one foot apart, toes pointing straight ahead, or very slightly outwards.   Imagine a chair behind you and that you are squatting down into it.   Go down to where the tops of the thighs are just below parallel to the floor.   Keep your head up (find a place high on the wall, and focus on it throughout the entire set).   Keeping your head up will open up the breathing pathway and help you maintain perfect form.   Keeping your back flat, lower yourself into the imaginary chair and squeeze back to the upright position.   Find the contraction point (just before locking out).   Pause for a split second, tense thighs and continue.   There is no need to actually lock out.   Keep an even up-down rhythm and imagine a coiled spring (again).   As you lower down, already begin to think about the spring pushing you back up.   Breathe once for each repetition.

Lunges (upper thigh separation).   If this is your first time with this exercise, use a broomstick; no weights at all.   It is essential to develop perfection of form and balance before struggling with added resistance. Start with the pole across the back of your shoulders, head up, feet slightly apart.   Work one side at a time.   Step forward (with your left foot) about two and a half feet. Keep the back leg as straight as possible.   Go onto the ball of the left foot, and flex the glute of the rear leg.   Spring back to the starting position.   Continue with the left leg for the full number of reps. After completion follow the same procedure with the right leg.

Leg extensions (middle and lower thigh separation).   Sit upright on the extension machine, head over hips, spine in alignment, hands holding bench side for more solid stance.   Place ankles under pads, raise legs upwards (emphasis on squeezing).   As legs straighten, hold the contraction for a split second.   Do not kick legs up with a jerking movement.   Perform slo-mo reps.   Later, with exercise form perfected, you will have earned the right to speed up your reps.

Leg curls (hamstrings).   Lie facedown on the leg-curl machine, hands holding the sides of the bench.   Hook heels under the pads and slowly raise both legs simultaneously.   Keep hips flat on bench throughout reps.   Hold head up.   As your feet close on your lower back, find the contraction and squeeze down for a brief second before slowly lowering the resistance.   Return to a completely _leg-straight position_ between each repetition.

Squat (start)

Squat (finish)

Lunges (start)

Lunges (finish)

Leg Extensions (start)

Leg Extensions (finish)

Leg Curls (start)

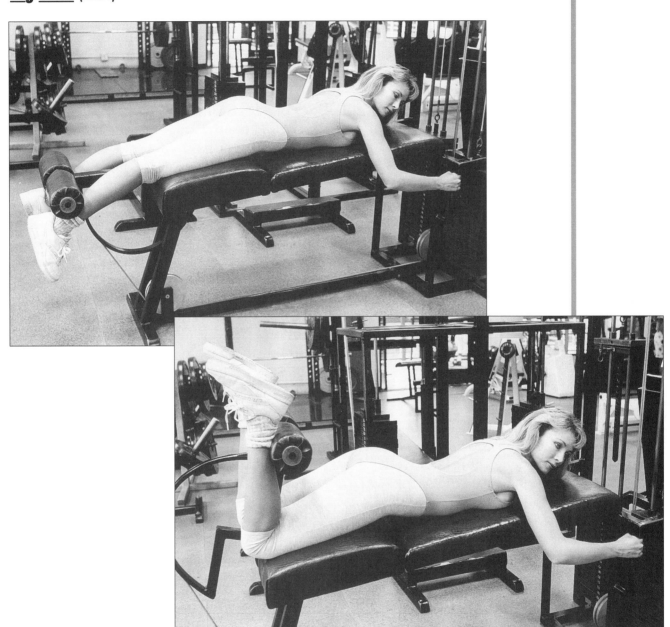

Leg Curls (finish)

Shoulders

Press behind neck (side shoulder). Take a moderately wide grip (when the upper arms are parallel to the floor the forearms are vertical). Keep the elbows back (arms in line with the shoulder girdle). Raise the bar up from behind the neck, pushing back with the elbows so that you feel a slight contraction in the deltoids. Use this contraction to squeeze the bar to the top of the movement. Make the deltoids squeeze the bar up. Concentrate on keeping this movement as a shoulder exercise, not an arm movement. The arms are accessories only to hold the bar in place. Stop a fraction of an inch short of locking out. To lock out in this movement is a cop-out.

Dumbbell side raise (shoulder width). This is a complicated movement to get right—few do it correctly. Stand upright, feet comfortably apart, palms facing each other, fingers interlaced in front of pelvic area. Bend the elbows slightly. Keeping fingers interlaced, attempt to press the elbows outwards and up. Square the shoulders off, and keep knees slightly bent. This is the action. The elbows are your key driving force. To better understand, imagine that you have an eye screw inserted in the top of your elbow attached to a string and, like a marionette, your elbow is being pulled upwards and lowered under control. . . . Now, using dumbbells, adopt the same reasoning. Keep hands limp (hooking the weight) and squeeze the deltoids as you raise. At the top of the movement always keep the palms down (imagine you are pouring liquid out of a soda bottle as you reach the arms-parallel position). Fight the weight on the downward path, concentrating the effect on the deltoids. You may perform this exercise in the standing or sitting position.

Upright row (front and side deltoid). This multijoint exercise gives a similar action to the side raise. Take a grip width of six to eight inches (palms facing pelvis); stand erect with feet comfortably apart. Imagine that marionette string on the outside of the elbow, lifting the elbow—not involving the arms. Raise the bar by squeezing the deltoids. Resist as the weight is lowered, again feeling it in the shoulders. As the bar reaches the neck area, find the contraction, pause and squeeze the elbows back. Lower.

Press Behind Neck (start)

Press Behind Neck (finish)

Dumbbell Side Raise (start)

Dumbbell Side Raise (finish)

__Upright__ __Row__ (start)

__Upright__ __Row__ (finish)

Biceps

Standing barbell curl (biceps and belly). Place your feet comfortably apart in an erect posture. Hold a barbell with hand spacing just slightly wider than shoulder width. Keep shoulders in a natural position, elbows just touching side of body. Before starting the curl, find the point of greatest contraction by bending the arms slightly. Pause and squeeze at this point. Find the biceps. Use the contraction. Then curl bar upwards slowly. No momentum. Keep the elbows at the side and hands in line with forearms (as though they were in splints). As the bar raises to chest, again find the second contraction, squeeze hard and lower.

Incline dumbbell curl (lower and middle biceps). Do not rest head back on bench. Keep it in a natural position off the bench. Use a sixty-degree angle. Hold two dumbbells by your side, palms facing inward (thumbs up). Begin by contracting the biceps and proceed to curling motion, elbows back. As the dumbbells begin to rise, rotate the hands to palms-up position. Keep hips down and back flat, and lift rib cage up. At the top of the movement allow the elbows to come forward no more than one inch. Find the contraction and squeeze it briefly before lowering weights.

Alternating dumbbell curl (belly of biceps). Sit or stand erect with feet comfortably apart, holding a dumbbell in each hand, at arms-down position by side (palms facing each other). Start curling the left-hand dumbbell upwards. Supinate (twist palm anticlockwise) as the dumbbell is lifted. Cross the hand over in front of the midchest to achieve the best contraction. Hold and squeeze. Lower to start position. Commence same procedure with right hand supinating in a clockwise direction. Alternate hands until completion of set.

Standing Barbell Curl
(start)

Standing Barbell Curl
(finish)

Incline Dumbbell Curl (start)

Incline Dumbbell Curl (finish)

Alternating Dumbbell Curl (start)

Alternating Dumbbell Curl (finish)

Triceps

Lying triceps extension (belly of triceps). Lie on a flat bench in a supine position (face up), feet flat on ground. Grasp a barbell in the center with hands eight to ten inches apart. Imagine that the elbows are tied in this position, i.e., eight to ten inches apart, with a rope. Lower the bar under control, slowly to the hairline. Your head should be slightly over the back of the bench. As the weight is lowered go for maximum triceps stretch, keeping elbows in. Let the triceps squeeze the weight back up to the near straight-arm position. Do not straighten right out to the resting point where the tension is taken off the triceps. Find the contraction, squeeze and lower.

Triceps bench dips (lower triceps). If as a beginner you find difficulty with this, you may place your feet on the floor for the first few workouts. Soon you will be able to place them on a bench as shown. Begin with hands outside hips in the arms-straight position, slightly unlocked so that the triceps are contracted. Keeping the body upright, lower to the point where the triceps are at maximum stretch. Return to the top combination without pause. Keep your head up throughout. If flexibility is a problem, try going lower each rep.

Triceps pushdown (entire triceps). Hold the pulley bar, elbows at your side. Contract the triceps before commencing the pushdown. Consciously use the triceps exclusively to extend the bar down to the near-locked position, so that the hands meet the frontal thigh. Find the belly of the triceps and squeeze. Keep a slo-mo, up-down rhythm going without leaning either back or forward and keeping elbows still throughout.

Lying Triceps Extension (start)

Lying Triceps Extension (finish)

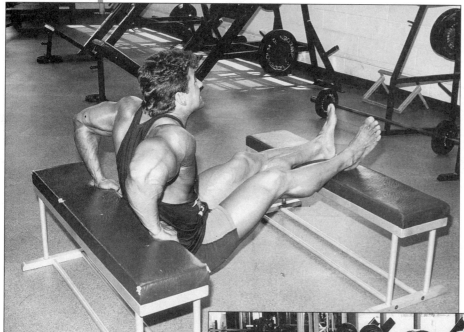

Triceps Bench Dips (start)

Triceps Bench Dips (finish)

Triceps Pushdown (start)

Triceps Pushdown (finish)

Calves

Standing calf raise (overall gastrocnemius). Ideally this should be done with a calf machine. If you do not have any specialized apparatus, use a loaded barbell across the back of your shoulders. Place your feet (parallel to each other six to eight inches apart) on a high block. Placing all the weight on the balls of your feet, stretch downward to the max with the heels. The block should be so high that your heels are never able to touch the floor. Begin by flexing the calf and then raise all the way up on the balls of your feet, lower and repeat. Maximum stretch in both directions is essential—no bouncing allowed.

Seated calf raise (soleus and lower calf). Use a seated calf machine when possible. Otherwise place a loaded barbell across knees (with adequate towels to supply padding). As in the previous exercise use a high block and go for maximum up-down stretch. No ballistic (bouncing) whatsoever. Avoid leaning back to cheat the weight up.

Leg-press calf raise (overall gastrocnemius). This is one of the best calf-stretching movements. Allow the toes to be forced down to their greatest stretch—the more flexibility you develop when stretching your calves, the better results you'll achieve from lower leg training. Keep the knees slightly bent, but don't overbend them to the extent that maximum stretch is lost. Press toes up to greatest height possible and lower to max slowly, deliberately seeking to keep in touch with the stretch throughout.

Standing Calf Raise (start)

Standing Calf Raise (finish)

Seated _Calf_ _Raise_ (start)

Seated _Calf_ _Raise_ (finish)

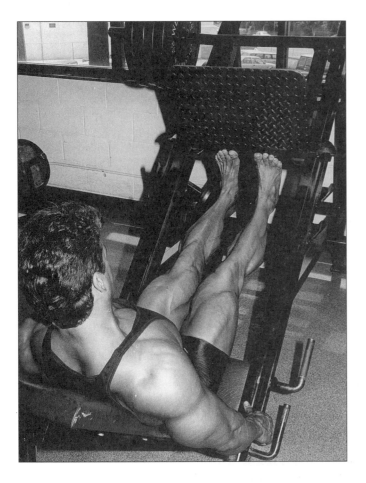

Leg-Press _Calf_ _Raise_ (start)

Leg-Press _Calf_ _Raise_ (finish)

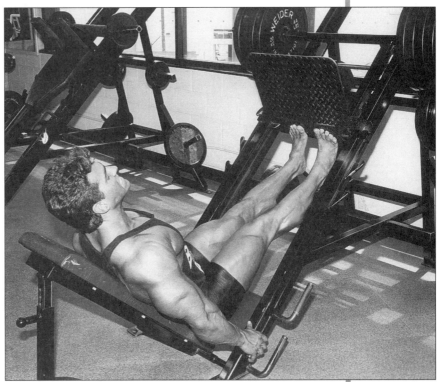

Abdominals

Lying leg raise (lower abdominals). Use the bench as indicated, knees slightly bent, back flat and pushed into the bench. Keeping the chin into the chest so that the body is slightly curled forward, raise legs in slo-mo style from six inches below parallel to six inches above parallel. Concentrate the effect into the lower ab muscles.

Crunches (middle and upper abdominals). Place yourself along a bench as shown, upper legs, knees and ankles together, hands behind head. Raise head toward ceiling, shortening length between thorax and pelvis (the function of the abs). If necessary use hands under hips to support lower back, but it is very important to push lower back into bench. In advanced stage you may lift feet off the bench so that thighs are vertical, legs crossed at ankles.

Added note: There are only two main functions for the abs—shortening the length of the torso and lifting the legs. Any variations of these two functions fall under leg raises (hanging, lying, etc.) and crunches (crunch, roman chair, sit-up, etc.). No matter what you see in the gym, perform no weighted side bends. The weighted reps will cause muscular growth leading to oversize oblique muscles (adding unwanted thickness to the waist). We are trying to add abdominal tone without mass.

Lying Leg Raise (finish)

Lying Leg Raise (start)

Crunches (start)

Crunches (finish)

BEGINNERS ROUTINE 1

	Sets	Reps
Warm-up		
Ten minutes stationary bike (moderate pace)		
Back		
Bent-over barbell row	2	15
Chest		
Flat bench press	2	20
Upper Legs		
Back squat	2	20
Lunges	2	20
Leg curls	2	15
Calves		
Standing calf raise	2	20
Shoulders		
Seated press behind neck	2	15
Biceps		
Incline dumbbell curl	2	15
Triceps		
Lying triceps extension	2	15
Abdominals		
Crunches	2	20

BEGINNERS ROUTINE 2

	Sets	Reps
Warm-up		
Moderate running in place (two minutes) only done to slightly elevate the pulse		
Chest		
Incline bench press	2	15
Back		
Wide-grip front pulldown	2	20
Hyperextension	2	15
Upper Legs		
Back squat	2	20
Leg extension	2	15
Leg curls	2	15
Calves		
Leg-press calf raise	2	20
Shoulders		
Upright row	2	15
Triceps		
Triceps pushdowns	2	15
Abdominals		
Lying leg raise	2	20

3

APPRENTICESHIP
TO
MASTERY

Knowledge is really nothing but experience.
—*Albert Einstein*

Most of the books you read about exercise are pretty dogmatic. They say, "You must do this, this and this to build your body." They don't consider your desires or abilities. They assume people are clones and that the same routines will work for everyone. Most of them drone on about how if you want to build your body you must do this routine for this many sets and this many repetitions. From one publication to the next these routines look remarkably similar. You might begin to think that just because of the sheer volume of nearly identical information, they might be correct. I'm here to tell you otherwise. Body-building is for the individual, and every individual is different.

So instead of rehashing the old dogma, let's begin to look at training from the individual standpoint. Body-building is about perfecting *your* individual potential. What you need to do is gather all the tools together that will enable you to do that.

The contents of this book are like a map and compass. They are tools to help you find the way. The map shows all the roads available for getting from point A to point B. The compass helps to make sense of those roads and to find direction along them. Only you know what your destination is. That destination is where you want your training to take you and what you want it to do for you. I realize that 99 percent of people who exercise have no intention of competing in a physique competition. That doesn't mean they don't want to harden their muscles, balance their development or become more fit and healthy. Body-building is one of those things that you can't cheat at. Both with respect to your nutritional intake, and your training routine, you only get back what you put in.

I'm all for building head-to-toe mass in order to give the impression of strength and power, but the size you build must be *intelligent mass.* You should never perform any exercise unless you know exactly what that exercise will do for your physical development. You must have a realistic blueprint in your mind of how you want to look. Every exercise you perform must be included in your routine only if it contributes to the fulfillment of your ultimate plan. If you lose sight of this, you'll join hands with the millions of other weight trainers who are merely going through the motions, with little real thought of how to build a truly positive body image.

As I've already pointed out, learning to build a body is very much like learning to build a house. The neophyte starts as an apprentice and works toward becoming a journeyman. With time, knowledge and experience, he'll eventually become a master carpenter.

As a beginning body-builder, you can quickly get to the stage where you're training correctly, but if you're going to be a real success you have to go through an apprenticeship. And this doesn't just apply to newcomers. Many people who've been working out for years have very little understanding of how to train optimally or how to direct their workout instincts toward positive results.

As an apprentice, you *must* begin with a structured routine. It's within this structure that you begin to learn how your body works. As you travel the road to mastery, you'll learn to let go of that structure and head toward an instinctive point in training where you'll have learned what works best for your needs.

But first you must absorb the lessons your body will be teaching you. For this, the training journal is invaluable. It will act as your information center, enabling you to review past workouts and recognize patterns of performance. Sooner or later these patterns will reveal that certain body parts aren't responding. You should react by becoming obsessed with the weak area. Explore every avenue of attack—fall in love with the muscle in question. Too many people "throw in the towel" when confronted by an underpar body part. Rather than fall in love with it, they try and forget it exists. You should learn the contraction of a weak area, determine with the help of an anatomy chart (*Gray's Anatomy* is one of the best books on the subject) the origins and insertions of the muscles involved, and seek out the precise action of the muscle. Does it help to move the arms upward? Sideways? Is any twisting involved? You can't learn too much about a weak muscle group. The body talks to us constantly. Part of reaching the mastery stage is listening to the body and learning how all the various techniques we use affect growth or nongrowth.

I've already mentioned that body-building is like sculpture. The barbells and dumbbells act as the artist's hammer and chisel. There's a contradiction here, though, because I actually see the body as something more like clay. When you use a hammer or chisel on wood or stone, you can only take away. If you see your body as sculpture in clay, you'll realize that you can use the tools of body-building to add and subtract mass. This is done by working certain areas harder with aggressively structured sets and repetitions, while merely toning other areas that you wish to "put on hold" until you've achieved an ideal balance. Let me give you an example. Years ago, Reg Park, a multi–Mr. Universe who competed in the sixties and seventies, became an insatiable bench presser. In fact, he was so adept at the movement that he became one of the first men in history, certainly the first body-builder, to bench-press 500 pounds. Aside from his love for bench pressing, Reg also performed a variety of mass-building exercises to build even more size in his pecs. Consequently, his pectorals were

huge and out of proportion with the rest of his body parts. Reg didn't need to be told that his pecs were too big. He ceased all bench pressing and other direct chest exercises altogether and just maintained chest tone, which came from the overlapping effect of such movements as wide-grip chins, pulldowns, pullovers and shoulder presses. As a result, his pectoral massiveness lessened until it was once again in perfect proportion to his shoulders, back, legs and every other body part. Even though he was a master of the sport, Reg Park knew that the learning process was ongoing. He realized that no one can ever know enough about perfecting his or her individual potential.

In my case I found that my thighs have a predisposition for massive size. I enjoy heavy, intense leg training, but if I get overenthusiastic my thighs can easily grow out of balance with the rest of my physique. Diligent training, however, has prevented this from happening.

It's taken nearly ten years for me to reach a place where I can call myself a master of this sport. I had to go through all the self-learning along the road from apprenticeship to mastery. I learned to use the map and compass of my acquired knowledge to find my way as an athlete. Another thing that I've learned is that mastery is not a constant state. The map is always changing. Your body never remains the same. So what worked in the past may not work now. It's a matter of constantly learning. Every time I turn around I learn something new, which I then integrate into my training.

Remember that the road to mastery is an individual one. The things you learn on that journey are dedicated to *your* growth and the realization of *your* potential. Many people become discouraged, feeling that their physical potential is not very good. They're intimidated by reading fitness magazines or by walking into a gym. It might be wise at such times to recall that we all start out as beginners. There will always be the memory of "the very first time I picked up a weight" in each body-builder's mind.

The physical gifts you were born with will only partly determine your success as an athlete. I divide the potential for athletic success into three key areas: genetics, work ethic and spirit.

Genetics play an important role in becoming a world-class athlete. It's said that world records are usually broken by athletes who possess great genetic ability. In body-building, a person with great genetic potential would have a high propensity for building muscle mass, an even distribution of muscle fibers throughout the body, low body fat, strong connective tissue and a skeletal frame that enhances proportion. Yet, probably 80 percent of all world-class body-builders are lacking in more than one of these areas. There are no perfect genetic specimens—especially in body-building, where the very people who are likely to take up the sport are those who perceive imperfections in themselves. The idea is to capitalize on your genetic strengths while you work to make up for any weaknesses.

The second key contributor to athletic success is *work*. It's only through a highly developed *work ethic* that you'll be able to create an ideal body. This means demonstrating the persistence to go in and do what is necessary to achieve your goals. If an athlete has great genetics but is lazy in the gym, he or she will only succeed on a very limited basis. Most genetically gifted but lazy athletes come to a roaring standstill, because they are trying to rest on their laurels. You can definitely make up for low genetic ability by just putting that proverbial nose to the grindstone. The best saying I know for reinforcing my own work ethic is: "Just do it now."

The third key ingredient is less tangible than the first two. You can look in the mirror and get a good idea of what your genetic potential is. Your sweat-soaked clothes and exhausted, accomplished feeling at the end of your workout will give you a good idea of your work ethic. Where does the *spark* come from, though? The work ethic is the machine that helps us achieve goals, but what is the catalyst that gets that machine up and running? I call it *spirit*. Spirit is the higher intelligence inside ourselves that we call on when making decisions. It's the ability to visualize and plan how to get from one place to another. I describe the proper use of spirit as "listening to your heart."

Hard work without higher purpose is just pragmatic emptiness. There are many people who work very hard at their jobs but wish they were somewhere else. The intense passion to accomplish a task is the fuel that puts the machine in motion. It is the athlete who succeeds in balancing genetics, work ethic and spirit who'll achieve mastery of the sport.

The best example of someone who's considered by "experts" in the sport to be lacking in genetic potential is Rich Gaspari. Rich, though, is driven by an incredible work ethic and spirit. By calling on these two ingredients, he's achieved a 100 percent package and has consistently beaten pros who possess what experts consider to be three to four times greater genetic potential. He is a true master of the sport of body-building.

4

•••••

INCREASING
THE
INTENSITY

•••••

Along the road from apprenticeship to mastery, you'll be using a large variety of exercise techniques. Most of these techniques are designed to increase the intensity of the workouts. *Intensity* is a word that gets used a great deal when discussing training. Intensity here means the level of work that you put into a set of an exercise. *When you're doing a set, the repetitions should be continued until the last one you complete is the last one you could possibly do.* The set should be performed using your own energy (no one is helping you lift the weight) in correct exercise style (not throwing or heaving the weight). I call this *positive failure.*

After warming up your muscles, you should be attempting to go to positive failure on every set of every exercise during your workout. The exceptions would be:

1. During your initial workouts as an absolute beginner.
2. When training an area that's recovering from an injury.
3. For the first few workouts when returning from an extended layoff.

During these periods, you should tailor your intensity to your body's needs. If you push to positive failure during your first beginning workouts, you could wind up, like I did, not being able to move for a week. It's far better to concentrate on the exercise form and to increase the intensity as your body adapts.

Adaptation plays an important role in your progress as a bodybuilder. In most cases your muscles will adapt to the work load you give them. It will be up to you to increase the intensity of that work load as your muscles adapt. That's why positive failure is so important. As your muscles grow stronger, you'll be able to push them harder. Positive failure does not mean stopping at the twelfth rep if you still have the ability to do three more. Your repetition goals are there to give you something to work toward. They are only the stopping points if you've reached positive failure. The intensity of a single exercise can be increased in the following ways:

1. Keeping the weight the same and increasing the intensity and duration of muscle contraction (squeezing and holding the rep).
2. Keeping the weight the same and increasing the number of reps until positive failure is achieved.
3. Increasing the weight and striving to do as many reps as before.

The following are exercise techniques that push your body beyond positive failure. These techniques are some of the tools you can use to achieve your potential. Please remember that you are working with a human body and not a machine. Every time you push your body beyond positive failure you *decrease* its ability to recover from the workouts, thereby *increasing* the length of time necessary for the trained body part to recuperate.

Intelligent, intuitive use of these tools can speed the progress toward your goals. Misusing them could leave you burnt out, overtrained and having to start again at square one.

F O R C E D   R E P S

A *forced rep* is a term used to explain a way of continuing a set after normal positive failure (failure to perform another repetition) is reached. A training partner lightly pulls up on the bar to enable you to pass the hardest part of an exercise (the sticking point) and continue to completion of the set. Take bench presses, for example. Your training partner will "help" you lift the bar "over the hump" for an additional couple of reps that you would otherwise not be able to achieve. Forced reps should be used only infrequently. If you used them on each exercise for every workout, you would be burned out within a week.

S P O T T I N G A N D
L I F T - O F F

Spotting and *lift-off* techniques are used to assist someone trying to take a set past positive failure. A *spot* involves helping your partner lift the weight when it becomes too heavy for him to complete the rep without assistance. Giving a spot does not mean lifting the weight for him. You're just trying to assist with the minimum amount of effort that will allow the rep to be completed. For example, on a barbell chest-pressing exercise, you would stand at the head of the bench while your partner did his or her set. In advance, visually plan where you'll put your hands if a spot is necessary. Look at the bar. The best place to hold the bar while spotting is just inside the area where the knurling ends on a standard olympic bar. The most important thing is to place your hands evenly so that you'll be lifting the bar in advance. There is nothing worse than having someone grab the bar off center. This can cause an accident or injury to the person doing the exercise. When your partner reaches positive failure and wants to push past, he should signal you by a look or grunt or by saying something like, "One more." It should be a communication that you both understand exactly. Then, take hold of the bar evenly and make sure that you have your balance. Lift up, relieving only enough of the pressure for the lifter to complete the rep. The greatest abuse I see of spotting is a bench presser who is using more weight than he can use correctly. He'll perform one rep and expect the training partner to lift the weight off his chest for nine or ten more reps. This person needs to put his ego aside, use a weight that he can handle and allow his training partner to do his or her lifting during his or her set.

If you're spotting someone doing a dumbbell-pressing movement, place your cupped hands under the person's elbow, hold tightly and not only help lift the weight, but also use your judgment to help the lifter balance it.

For squatting, you should stand directly behind your partner and as the set reaches positive failure, wrap your arms up under his arms and around his chest for support. Have your feet firmly planted in a medium-wide stance. Now squat down with your partner and the spot will come as you raise back up with him. You'll basically be doing a squat also;

just hang on to his body to help support him in completing the rep. You can also exert a slight pressure backward to help your partner stay upright if he's leaning forward on the spotted rep.

The term *lift-off* is used to describe the act of helping your partner lift the loaded bar off the rack at the start of the set. For example, when giving someone a lift-off on the bench press, you would grab the bar in the same position as giving a spot. When the partner signals, you'll assist him in lifting the bar into place. This is usually done when the bar is too heavy for the trainer to move into position on his own. At the conclusion of the set you can assist your partner in reracking the weight.

C O M P O U N D   S E T S

A variety of methods fall under this heading. Alternating two exercises for the same body part without rest is a *bi-set;* three exercises is a *tri-set;* and four or more exercises for a body part is a *giant set.*

I believe strongly in using these methods for my own precontest training. Usually I alternate workouts of straight sets with workouts of tri-sets and giant sets.

Three of the more effective methods for overcoming body-part sticking points are as follows:

Tri-Set Hamstrings Routines

Lying leg curl

Stiff-leg deadlift

Standing one-leg curl

Giant Set Shoulder Routines

Dumbbell side raise

Press behind neck

Bent-over side raise

Upright rowing

Tri-Set Front Thigh Routines

{
Extensions

Squats

Sissy squats[a]

Tri-Set Front Thigh Routines

{
Extensions

Leg press (toes straight)

Ballet squat (performed with the toes pointing outward at a 180-degree angle)

[a] A description of this exercise follows in text.

A *sissy squat* is *a* freehand exercise used to fully stretch the front thigh. Stand with your feet six to twelve inches apart, toes pointing forward. Holding on to a stationary piece of equipment for balance, raise up on your toes. Instead of squatting straight down as if sitting in a chair, stretch down so that your feet remain stationary and your knees almost touch the floor out in front of you. When raising and lowering your body, your hips should be pushed as far forward as possible, giving your body an arched appearance with the front of the hips being the most forward part of the arch. Flex the thighs at the top of the movement and find the maximum stretch at the bottom.

It's nearly impossible to perform giant sets in a crowded gym, because it's vital that you move from one exercise to another with a minimum of rest. Only when you have completed one cycle of four or five exercises can you take a brief two-minute breather. The correct way to work with compound sets is to arrange your exercise stations in advance. They should be loaded up with the correct poundages, ready to go. When working the arms or shoulders with compounds, I set up all my dumbbells at different sites (not too far apart). After one movement is completed I go straight to the next area, take a couple of breaths and get right into the next set. Keep moving and make your compounds work. The theory is that growth is stimulated by pushing greater and greater amounts of blood through the muscle while working all the different angles and aspects.

DESCENDING SETS

Theoretically this method (also known as *down the rack*, *stripping* or *triple-drop*) is one of the most workable because the early reps of a set, the easy ones, are not wasted. Every part of the set becomes demanding. A descending set entails the reduction of weight while the set itself is being performed. Instead of just the latter part of a set being difficult, a descending set will have three "difficult" areas. All this translates into more intensity.

To illustrate this method, let's take the press behind neck. Start with the barbell loaded with sufficient weight to allow four or five good contraction reps. When you can't perform any more, have two workout partners simultaneously remove about 20 percent of the weight (usually a ten- or fifteen-pound disc from either side) and continue performing reps until you once more reach a point of failure. Have your partners remove another 20 percent of the load. Press out the weight until you can't do another rep.

It's important that the discs be removed slowly and simultaneously—otherwise the balance of the bar will be affected. Continue as soon as the discs are removed. No resting. With a little imagination, this principle can be used in just about every exercise. Some trainers using selectorized weight stacks downsize their own weights by pulling the pin and inserting it themselves. This is acceptable, but it's still better to keep the rhythm intact by having a training partner make the change.

Descending sets are grueling. You are, in effect, tripling your intensity, so a reduction in the overall number of sets may be in order.

SUPERSETS

Supersets (alternating two different exercises of opposing muscle groups, i.e., biceps/triceps or quads/hamstrings) are a popular way of exercising when one is seeking a quick workout and a maximum pump. There's no doubt that time is saved when you superset as opposed to performing straight sets, because supersets are carried out with the minimum amount of rest between sets. A typical superset would be alternating barbell curls (biceps) and lying extensions (triceps).

Supersets may also help overall definition because their nonstop performance may hype up the metabolic rate and slightly increase the fat-burning process. Some people appear to rush their supersets, even to the point of bouncing their reps up and down like a piston. I feel this is wrong. Remember: You should be striving to "feel" the muscle and to work to positive failure. Any "quickness" should be limited to moving from one exercise to another.

PREEXHAUST

The *preexhaust method* is designed to stress the muscles to the maximum by alternating two preselected exercises: one an isolation movement, the second a combination movement. Let's take some common torso exercises to illustrate this method. When you perform bench presses for the pectoral (chest) muscles, the triceps of the arms are also involved, and because they're a smaller (weaker) muscle group they tend to tire before the pectorals. The preexhaust system helps combat this situation, in this case by pretiring or exhausting your pectoral muscles before you perform the bench press. All that's necessary is that you do a set of flyes immediately before going to the bench press. The flyes don't work the arms at all, just the pecs. The result is that, when you perform the bench press, the triceps will be strong enough to easily cope with the exercise, while the pectorals, already tired, will be stressed even more severely.

Let's use another example: the deltoids. When you perform the press behind neck exercise, it's often difficult to really pump up the shoulders because the weaker triceps tend to give out first. Answer?

Work the shoulders with an isolation exercise first, one that doesn't involve the arms. The dumbbell side raise is a good example. Perform a set of these and then immediately follow up with a set of presses behind the neck. Now you'll really feel those shoulders burn.

Here is a complete preexhaust routine.

	Sets	Reps
Shoulders		
Isolation Movement		
Dumbbell side raise	3	12
Combination Movement		
Press behind neck	3	10
Chest		
Isolation Movement		
Flat bench flye	3	10
Combination Movement		
Flat bench press	3	8
Front Thighs		
Isolation Movement		
Leg extensions	3	12
Combination Movement		
Squat	3	10
Hamstrings		
Isolation Movement		
Leg curl	3	12

	Sets	Reps
Combination Movement		
Stiff-leg deadlift	3	15
Back		
Isolation Movement		
Across-bench pullover	3	12–15
Combination Movement		
Wide-grip pull-ups	3	8–12
Biceps		
Isolation Movement		
Bench preacher curl	3	10
Combination Movement		
Narrow undergrip pull-up	3	12–15
Triceps		
Isolation Movement		
Triceps pushdowns	3	12
Combination Movement		
Parallel-bar dips	3	10
Forearms		
Isolation Movement		
Reverse wrist curl	3	12
Combination Movement		
Reverse barbell curl	3	15

CHEATING REPS

I prefer to use the term *loose exercise style* rather than *cheating. . . .* It sounds less criminal. You'll note that I've stressed over and over again the importance of "feeling" the reps, of "finding" the contraction each time you flex during an exercise, so why even give the time of day to a method such as cheating? It's all in the execution. The beginning body-builder cheats (uses loose exercise style) to make a set *easier* on the muscles. However, an advanced-level body-builder can use the cheating principle creatively to make a set *harder*. Simply avoid cheating before you've absolutely taken your set to failure. When this happens you can inject the minimum of added body motion (hip thrusting, torso swaying, etc.), to get past the point beyond which you previously couldn't move. Now you can again use your muscle power to complete the repetition at hand.

The other valid point about creative cheating is that it enables you to utilize negative reps. For example, if you cheat the weight up (in the standing press, curl, etc.) you're in a position to lower it slowly, so that the muscle benefits from the negative resistance. Exercise physiologists long ago concluded that the negative (downward) half of a resistance exercise offers at least as much value in contributing to mass and power development as the positive (upward) half.

CIRCUIT TRAINING

Circuit training is a method popular with many different kinds of athletes. It can't be performed in a crowded gym unless the gym is set up to cater to circuit trainers exclusively. The circuit method requires setting up twelve to fifteen exercise stations, each working a different muscle group, and then having trainers perform one set only of each in succession. As a general rule, trainers don't perform two exercises in a row for the same muscle area. You perform the routine by moving from station to station, with no more than fifteen to twenty seconds' rest between exercises. Several circuits (two to five) may be perfomed. The following is a sample routine:

Exercise	Sets	Reps
Standing dumbbell press (shoulders)	1	12
Wrist curl (forearms)	1	15
Hyperextension (lower back)	1	20
Standing calf raise (lower legs)	1	25
Bench press (chest)	1	10
Leg curl (hamstrings)	1	15
Parallel-bar dips (triceps)	1	15–20
Crunches (abdominals)	1	20
Leg extension (front thighs)	1	15
Undergrip chin (biceps)	1	10–15
Seated pulley row (back)	1	12
Incline dumbbell bench press (chest)	1	12
Upright row (shoulders)	1	12

Going from apprenticeship to mastery can be an exciting journey. But remember that you want to discover which principles, foods, disciplines and frequency systems work best for you. In all probability you'll find that most methods work to some extent and that no single system should be used in isolation. Quite often one principle, such as *straight sets,* works well for a while, and then with a change—to *compound sets*, for example—a new growth plateau is achieved. After a while progress may again slow down, only to start once more when you turn to the *preexhaust system* or *supersets*. You need constant variety and change to keep your workout fresh. Don't stick with any one method (with the possible exception of straight sets).

On the other hand, you could find that certain systems just don't suit your temperament or level of tolerance for strenuous exercise. If this is so, then your experimentation has proven valuable. The learning process, along with journal notes, will guide you in discovering which methods suit your needs.

Competing with Chris Dickerson.

5

•••••

BALANCE, VARIETY, FEEL

•••••

Body-building is just a slice of life. After all, there are other pursuits, pastimes and such. But I believe if a thing is worth doing it's worth doing well.

There are three main components to my training philosophy. With each I associate a specific word that sums up my approach.

•••

BALANCE

The first of these words is *balance*. You can't set realistic goals unless your priorities are in order. What are your family or spousal commitments? Do you have children or animals to care for? How demanding is your job?

It's important that you meet these questions head-on and decide where body-building fits into your lifestyle. You may be reading this book simply because you want to build a well-shaped, toned body. But if your desire is to compete, you'll have to put body-building (workouts, recuperation and nutrition) before *anything* else. This might mean curtailing other sporting activities, putting a temporary hold on your social calendar or dropping a second job needed to buy a new car. Are you willing to pay the price?

Understand that both the *shape trainer* and the body-builder have to follow my training principles to reach their goals. Both will need to practice good dietary habits, get sufficient sleep and follow a systematic approach. But a shape trainer can afford to train less frequently and for shorter durations of time, take off the odd day even though it's a day scheduled for a workout and generally allow the mind to relax more. A would-be competitor, on the other hand, will have to make a contract with himself that spells out dedication with a capital D. He'll have to drop personal habits that limit progress—for example, partying on a regular basis and all the things that are associated with that lifestyle (e.g., smoking, drinking, drugs, lack of sleep).

Balance also refers to the physique itself. How do your arms compare to your chest? Are your legs underdeveloped in relation to your torso? It's common for beginning body-builders (especially home trainers) to ignore the legs and just train the upper body and arms. Let's face it, leg work *is* tough. Squatting up and down with a heavy weight on your back is okay for the first few reps, but the last ones are . . . *sheer pain!* We all know the story of Joe with the big arms who struts around the gym in a tight T-shirt, works only his upper body and arms and is always clad in tight jeans that cover matchstick-size legs. Be careful taking this guy to the beach, because he'll sink into the sand and you'll lose him. Joe needs to find balance in his training.

Similarly, when you have an underpar area, or a body part that isn't responding well to training, you have to put more thought into building up that area. You need to overconcern yourself with the weak body part: study it, feel it, read about it and train it vigorously, using every intelligent principle you can muster. As I've said before, you need to fall in love with your weak area, dwelling on it to such an extent that you build a whole new motivation to bring it up to par. Merely performing a couple of extra exercises for an underdeveloped body part won't get the job done.

Even identifying your weaknesses may be a problem if you're wedded to a certain perception of yourself. I've met people with great calves who feel they are quite lacking in that area. Some with superb abdominal development simply don't recognize it, while others whose muscles are floating in a sea of fat feel they are ripped to the bone. If you're unsure how you stack up, ask a friend for his opinion. But I offer two cautions:

1. The friend must be absolutely honest in appraising your body.
2. The friend must be knowledgeable about what constitutes a well-balanced physique.

In the sixties and seventies body symmetry and proportion didn't figure highly in physique judges' evaluations. Rather, it was mass and cuts. A balanced physique was a bore. Everyone seemed to want the freaky look. "Wow! Look at his thighs, man. They must be thirty-five inches." "Man, see them pecs. They look more like mountains." "Gee, that guy's great. He's got veins popping out all over his body." You know what I'm talking about: the fans needed flash and glitz. They wanted freaks. Sure, proportion and balance were beautiful, but they were a yawn.

Thank goodness we're returning to sensible body-building. Maximum size and cuts are still desired, yes, but so too is dignity. Today, most top competitors train in line with what their instincts tell them the human body should look like. They train in a balanced fashion to achieve a balanced physique.

VARIETY

The second component of my training philosophy can best be summed up by the word *variety*. Again, there's a multiple meaning intended here.

First, variety refers to the need to incorporate other things into your life besides body-building. Sure, if you're competing you have to turn your thoughts inward, especially during the last weeks of preparation, but the sport should never be allowed to consume your every waking moment. Develop interests in auto mechanics, hiking, music, gardening, home improvement, film, theater or reading. ("Hey, whaddya give me dis magazine for? Ain't nuttin' 'bout muscles in it!")

Okay, so you can't go to football practice before your workout—or dancing afterwards—and expect to become Mr. Olympia, but I've seen a lot of young body-builders throw themselves entirely into the sport of body-building, neglect their other interests, give up their relationships, ostracize their families and lose their jobs . . . all to gain a couple of inches on their arms. And the irony is that their single-mindedness was so intense they flushed themselves down the drain. The very thing they'd committed themselves to wholeheartedly ended up strangling them. Take my word for it: your mental processes need more than one kind of stimulation.

Now, in the gym, variety applies in a couple of other ways. First, the exercises themselves should be substituted for each other frequently. The body thrives on change and diversity. Typically, it takes only about three workouts for the body to become totally familiar with a routine, so while there are some body-builders around, even good ones, who hardly change their routines at all from one year to the next, those who do incorporate liberal substitution will progress far faster.

Motivation to keep going to the gym and training with vision and enthusiasm is vital. If you perform the same old routine week after week, year after year, you have nothing to look forward to. You could work blindfolded. "Okay, we start with bench presses, then flyes, then cable crossovers . . . yawn." It's like eating cold oatmeal every morning. You need to spice things up.

Every exercise you perform "hits" the body in a different way, and as I've said, our muscles thrive on change. There are different aspects to every muscle group, and by changing an angle of a bench or steering a weight through a different arc, you can stimulate new areas into growth. A whole new set of fibers are stimulated when you change the order and selection of exercises. It's when you don't change things around that you develop the *basic body*—the kind power lifters have—good bulk but very little muscle symmetry or separation.

Over the years I've developed an armory of exercises for each body part—tried and tested movements that I consider to be of the best quality. There are, of course, literally hundreds of weight-training exercises, but your personal armory should consist of approximately ten to fifteen exercises per body part. They should be listed in the front of your training journal to remind you of the options you have. When I go into the gym for my workout, using my journal as my information center, I'll select two, three or four exercises (depending on how many movements I'm going to do for that body part), and then the next time I work that area, I'll make a different selection. Sometimes only angles will change (I might want to perform a thirty-degree-incline bench press instead of a forty-five degree). At other times the exercises will change drastically. Remember that the same type of equipment, if built by a different manufacturer, often gives a different effect. Depending on brand name, calf machines, pec-decks, crossover pulley machines, leg-extension machines and leg-press machines vary in the way they work your body. Take advantage of the wide variety of equipment that's available. Use your imagination and experience to discover new ways to keep your workout variety high. It goes without saying, of course, that you shouldn't use a different piece of equipment just because it's there. Many gyms have junky equipment that nobody uses because it's just not effective.

Right now you might be saying to yourself that you like certain exercises for each body part and don't feel you'd like to change them each time you work out. That's fine. If you have the motivation to really improve yourself with each exercise, use these movements for a while, but don't train with the same exercises for months or years because even though your motivation may remain high you'll still be depriving your muscle of being "hit" from a large variety of angles. Give thought to alternating two completely different workouts, and remember to keep an account of everything in your journal. It will prove to be your most valuable training partner.

I also stress variety in talking about number of repetitions. Up until now there've been two schools of thought in body-building:

1. Use sets of *low* reps and *heavy* weights to build a massive physique.

2. Use *higher* reps with *moderate* weights to push lots of blood through the muscle to build a massive physique.

If you've been training for a while, I'm sure you've tried both these methods and are aware that each gives a different feel to the muscles being worked. So which one is best?

The answer is *both*. Don't misunderstand me. I'm not advocating using both high and low reps to "play it safe," but rather because each system has a very real effect on building muscle mass. For the most part, you'll want to train within a range of six to twenty-five repetitions. (Using a rep-count of less than six doesn't contribute to the advanced development of skeletal muscles; the effect is more to exercise the tendons.) Occasionally, though, you'll want to use more than twenty-five repetitions, such as when you're working on the front thighs or abdominals.

Let's take a look at each of the three standard repetition ranges. Using the first range, six to nine, you'll strengthen the tendons, the ligaments, and the tie-ins of the muscles to connective tissues, thereby decreasing the chance of tears and injuries. Using the second range, ten to fifteen, you'll work the muscle belly more directly. With practice, substantial weights can still be used in this repetition range, but always bear in mind that stretching and contracting are more important than heaving and bouncing.

The higher repetition range, until recently, has been relatively unexplored. It's a range that most body-builders choose to ignore: "I don't do high reps because I hate sissy weights," some will say. Of course, this could be a disguised response, when the real reason is that *high reps burn and hurt like hell!*

Usually at about the twelfth to fifteenth rep, a deep burn sets into the muscles. Sometimes fibers start to fire off like fresh eggs in a frying pan. Most often these are *endurance fibers,* mitochondrial filaments that are stimulated by higher repetition movements (in concert with substantial resistance). At the same time the capillary system creates new pathways to feed new muscle growth. Without high repetitions these muscle-building activities couldn't commence.

● ●

FEEL

The third major component of my body-building philosophy can best be summarized by the word *feel*. Walk into any gym in the world and you'll see someone slinging a barbell around, performing a curl without the faintest idea of what he's doing. He's just trying to heave as much weight as possible, grunting and groaning, giving himself a hernia trying to get the weight up. He'll be lucky if he doesn't sling a biceps against the wall like a string of spaghetti. Basically, the whole point of body-building is *muscular contraction*. If, as they say, there's a "secret of the champs," that's it! So it's no secret anymore, is it? One more time: *If you don't feel the muscle, you can't grow the muscle.*

Young men often buy into societal pressure to be macho and to compete on the gym floor. Many times, women, who're pressured in a different way, concentrate more on good exercise form than on trying to lift maximum weights. All trainers need to learn that if they hang their ego at the door, they can achieve ego-satisfying goals as a result (i.e., the perfected physique).

Feeling the contraction is one of the most important aspects of body-building. That's why I tell beginners to perform rehearsal workouts (using extremely light weights, perfect slo-mo form and high repetitions) to open up the muscle-mind pathways and foster an awareness of muscle-contraction points.

One question I'm always asked in my seminars is: "Bob, do you believe in using heavy weight?" Yes, I do, but I have to qualify my answer by stating that I consider a weight "heavy" if the final repetition of a set is the last one you can possibly complete. Whether you're performing six repetitions or twenty-five, it's a matter of intensity. If you're pushing yourself to maximum on a set of twenty-six reps, then that becomes a heavy weight. The same goes for a set of six reps.

You *must* avoid thinking of weights as either heavy or light. Heavy versus light is a false dichotomy that leaves many trainers feeling either intimidated or dismissive and that causes them to adopt a program lacking in at least one important respect. Properly applied, every poundage has a use.

And remember: *balance, variety and feel* is your personal code to becoming *Beyond Built!*

• • • • •

6

THE
JOURNAL

• • • • •

I believe everything starts with a thought—an inspiration, if you like. If you're to achieve anything worthwhile, you must visualize your goals . . . and write them down.

Whether you wind up an Olympia winner, president of a huge corporation, or a bum with a bottle of rubbing alcohol hanging out of your hand often depends on goal-setting in the early years of adulthood. No one holds his level of achievement on a constant plane. If you're not moving in a positive direction, you're moving in a negative direction. Life never stands still. You have to set goals for yourself and continue to strive for positive results.

At a very young age Arnold Schwarzenegger wrote down what he wanted to accomplish in his life. He made a list. It went something like this:

• I want to be the greatest body-builder of all time.
• I want to live in America.
• I want to be a star in English-speaking films.
• I want to be financially secure for life.

Well, as you know, one by one Arnold achieved his goals. It took time, but he devoted all his energies to each task until he achieved it. Learn Arnold's lesson well. Most people have scattered, half-formed goals in their minds. This is not good enough—you must have aspirations that you can identify precisely, and you must strive to achieve them with single-minded determination.

All right, now, take the first page of your journal (a spiral notebook will nicely fit the purpose) and make a two-column list. Stand in front of a full-length mirror and record in one column your strengths and in the other your weaknesses. Remember that what you jot down will dictate the approach you'll take in your training. Start with your posture. Turn sideways. Have you got rounded shoulders? Does your head tilt forward? Now from the front—is one shoulder higher than the other? Are your collar bones horizontal to the floor, or do they rise much higher at the shoulder? Breathe in: "Show" your rib cage—is it a good size, with an expansive wide arch at the base? Or is it pinched in with a small arch? Look at your shoulders. Are they naturally wide, narrow or normal?

How's the muscle mass? How's the shape? Flex your biceps. Do they rise from your upper arm with a pleasant-looking full crest? Or do they resemble a short knot high up the arm near the shoulder? Are your biceps flat and peakless?

While in the flexed position, check out the triceps. Do they appear to have plenty of belly to them, a full curve right from elbow to armpit?

Forearms: Does the muscle start to rise near the wrist or do you have "long" wrists like a bowling pin, with development only around the elbow? The latter is the sign of an ectomorphic (skinny) frame.

Now, let's size up your chest. The development you have right now is not important—anyone can build pecs. It's the shape that counts, especially the shape of the lower pec line. Does it run straight across (ideal but rare) or are your pecs rounded at the base?

Abdominals. Are you lucky enough to have straight rows? Again, very few have, but it's nice if they do happen to be lined up neatly. Look at the region near the navel. Do you have the same development here as you do higher up?

Your legs. Is there sufficient development in the lower thigh to balance the mass in the upper-thigh area? Are your calves full-bellied and low, or high with a tiny knot of muscle near the knee? You will need to adjust your training strategies accordingly.

Turn sideways—check out those hamstrings. Do you have any? Okay, let's get to work. Your job now is to make a short analysis at the bottom of the page. Write down what you need to improve during the time period of this journal. This is important because not only have you started a record book of your analysis, but you have also *made a contract* with yourself to train in the most perfect way you know. Remember that though some of your structural "flaws" may be unchangeable, by working for intelligent mass you can create *your* ultimate body look.

On the second page of your notebook write down your goals. Begin with your long-term goals—in other words, where you *see* yourself in one year's time. Be realistic. Now move selectively down to the short-term goals. Two months' time, one month's time. If you've only been training three months, don't dream up wild, unattainable situations like becoming Mr. Olympia. It can be hard, but be as realistic as you can and only write down achievable goals. It's unreasonable to expect to put two inches on your arms in a month (unless you're training back to a previously held level, in which case it can be a cinch).

Years ago, I saw that story about Arnold in *Rolling Stone* magazine, took it around to my grandparents and all my friends and said, "I'm going to look like this in six months." Well, it took me considerably longer, so it was an unrealistic statement, but it sure fueled my goal system. By telling people my aspirations I'd not only made a verbal contract with an over-enthusiastic Bob Paris but I'd bared my wildest secret wishes to the world, putting myself in a vulnerable position. Now I *had* to follow through on my boast or else invite scorn and ridicule for my failure. I didn't do it in six months, but I *did* do it eventually, and my rise in the body-building world was interpreted as meteoric. My goal-setting plan was off in timing, but I *had*

laid out a positive plan of approach and gone all out to achieve it. The secret, of course, is to set realistic goals that are still ambitious enough to provide inspiration. Look at your long-term goal as a yardstick. The short-term goals are every inch along its length. Gain each inch deliberately and with total confidence and eventually you'll close in on your long-term goal.

During those times when I've been most successful I've also practiced strong visualization. I would compose a mental image, often fuzzy at first, like an out-of-focus photograph, but in time the image would become very strong. You can't expect to imagine things as clearly as a *Life* magazine cover or as logically (in terms of sequence) as a movie. But the more you practice, the clearer will be the visualization. *See* your training being accomplished with perfect form. Don't just imagine a glossy 8x10 of your physique as you want it to be; *see* yourself in a movie loop as soon as possible. Imagine yourself completing your goals one by one, always within the limits of your own structure and your own potential. Don't see your head on Bob Paris' body—see your head on your body, built to the max. If you are five feet tall, with stocky hips and narrow shoulders, don't visualize yourself as duplicating Lee Haney's physique. You're setting yourself up for failure, and subconsciously you're telling yourself that your own body is not good enough to be physically impressive. See your *own* body developed to the level you desire.

What I like to do, especially during the peaking phase before a competition, is to find a quiet place—usually the bedroom—and sit on a chair, either first thing in the morning or late at night. I take a deep breath and relax every part of my body. I follow with five or six more breaths, and by that time my mind and body are completely relaxed. I'm breathing myself down—way, way down. It's unbelievable how cluttered the mind becomes during the course of a day, so this quiet time comes as a relief.

For both the competitor and the noncompetitor, this relaxation ritual can be tremendously useful. When you've achieved serenity, run the following movie loop through your mind. *See* yourself as a success during an onstage presentation at an important contest; *strain* your ears to hear the applause. This mental release will actually manifest itself in concrete results; it's been shown time and time again in studies of athletes from all fields of endeavor. Those who use mental-rehearsal techniques are inevitably the most successful.

Another visualization aid I use is index cards. Any office-supply store carries them. During your quiet time, write on each one a very positive suggestion, in the present tense. "I am very disciplined with my diet." "I am Ohio's best body-builder." "I feel the full contraction for every rep I do in the gym." Keep these cards in your pocket, held together with a rubber band, and three or four times a day take them out, flick through them and stop and think about the especially important ones, *feeling* the accomplishment with every fiber of your body. Reviewing the cards takes no more than two minutes, but those two minutes are totally positive, enormously reinforcing and always packed with emotion. The positive-statement cards can be a natural extension of your journal, the part that you can carry around in your pocket. What follows are sample pages from my own personal journal (notice that I record sets, reps, poundages, and anything else I consider relevant).

Focus!!

[11:15 AM - 12:35 PM] FRONT THIGH, HAMSTRINGS, LOW BACK

FRONT THIGH

WARM-UP EXTENSIONS   1) 40^{30}_{30} 2) 40^{30}_{30}

TRI-SET [EXTENSIONS   1) 50^{30}_{30} 2) 50^{25} 3) 50^{25} 4) 50^{20}
45° LEG PRESS 45 LB. PLATES 1) 8 PLATES^{30} 2) 10^{25} 3) 10^{20} 4) 10^{20}
BACK SQUAT   1) 135^{xx} 2) 225^{8} 3) 315^{12} 4) 315^{12}

HAMSTRING, LOW BACK

STANDING ONE LEG CURL 1) 30^{25} 2) 35^{20} 3) 40^{15} 4) 40^{15}
BI-SET [STIFF LEG DEADLIFT 1) 135^{23} 2) 185^{20} 3) 225^{15} 4) 225^{15}
LYING LEG CURL 1) 60^{30} 2) 70^{22} 3) 70^{22} 4) 70^{21}
HYPEREXTENSIONS BODY-WEIGHT 1) ✓ 35 2) ✓ 35 3) ✓ 32 4) ✓ 36

USED VERY PUMPED IN FR. THIGH ; KNEES TIGHT WHEN I BEGAN HAMSTRINGS
SHOULD WAIT LONGER BETWEEN F. THIGH AND HAMS.
BEGAN WORKOUT TIRED NOT MUCH SLEEP LAST NIGHT BUT GOT
MOVING REAL WELL.

WOKE UP KIND OF EARLY THIS A.M.   WENT TO MUSEUM OF ART YESTERDAY -
GREAT! DROVE BACK IN RAIN   RENTED VIDEOS AND STAYED IN
BED 12:15   ACTIVE MIND DURING NIGHT. COULDN'T SLEEP.

AEROBICS] STAIR MACHINE   20 MIN 75%   AT GYM.

SUNDAY CONT.

SATURDAY   NO WORKOUT - REST DAY
          DAY OFF DIET

SUNDAY	NUTRITION		MULTI-AMINOS
MEAL#1 9:00 AM	3 WHOLE EGGS - FRIED IN PAM BOWL OF OATS & RAISINS		✓ 4 BEFORE MEAL ✓ 4 AFTER WORKOUT
MEAL#2 1:00 PM	PROTEIN/CARB. DRINK 2 TBSP. PROTEIN, BANANA FRESH STRAWBERRIES, WATER		
MEAL#3 3:30 PM	10 OZ FLANK STEAK 6 OZ PASTA STEAMED TOMATOES & GARLIC		✓ 4 BEFORE MEAL
MEAL#4 7 PM	6 OZ CHICKEN BREAST 2 CUPS RICE SM LETTUCE, TOMATOE SALAD WITH - LEMON & VINEGAR		✓ 4 BEFORE MEAL

MONDAY
CONT.

NUTRITION

MULTI-AMINOS

MEAL #1
6:45 AM
2 WHOLE EGGS + 4 EGG WHITES
LG. BOWL OATS
MED BANANA
✓ 4 BEFORE MEAL

MEAL #2
10:15 AM
10 RICE CRACKERS
LG. RED APPLE
✓ 4 AFTER WORKOUT

MEAL #3
11:30 AM
8 OZ VERY LEAN ROUND STEAK
2½ CUPS RICE
CARROT STICKS
✓ 4 BEFORE MEAL

MEAL #4
3:00 PM
1 CUP NONFAT YOGURT   MIXED WITH
½ CUP RICE
✓ 4 BEFORE MEAL

MEAL #5
7:00 PM
10 OZ TURKEY BREAST
2 LG BAKED POTATOES
STEAMED BROCCOLI
✓ 4 BEFORE MEAL

(A WINNER NEVER QUITS —
A QUITTER NEVER WINS!)

MONDAY
FEB. 5 1990
NIGHT OF CHAMP. 102
MR. D.   228 DAYS

8:15 - 9:45 AM (CHEST, SHOULDERS)

BODYWEIGHT 249½

CHEST

		1)	2)	3)	4)
INCLINE BARBELL PRESS	MED.GRIP TO NECK	135 ²⁵	225 ¹⁸	315 ⁹	315 ⁷
DIPS (FOR CHEST)	BODYWEIGHT	BW ¹⁶	BW ¹⁴	BW ¹⁵	BW ¹²
INCLINE FLYES		60 ²⁰	70 ¹⁰	80 ⁸	80 ⁹
ACROSS BENCH PULLOVER		80	90	90 ¹⁵	
CABLE CROSSOVER	STANDING UPRIGHT	30 ³⁵	40 ²⁵	40 ²⁰	

VERY GOOD SQUEEZES , GREAT PUMP ; FELT VERY STRONG SO DECIDED ON LOWER REPS FOR
B.B. PRESSES   INTENSE BURN ON HI-REPS   PUSHED LIMIT!!

SHOULDERS

		1)	2)	3)	4)
ONE ARM PULLEY SIDE RAISE		25 ²⁰@	25 ²⁰@	25 ²⁰@	
SEATED BARBELL PRESS BEHIND NECK		115 ¹⁰,¹⁰	135 ¹⁰	155 ⁸	185 ⁷
DOWN RACK D.B. SIDE RAISE		40,30,20 ²⁰	45,35,25 ⁷	50,40,30 ⁸	
SEATED BENTOVER S.R.		35 ¹²	40	45 ¹⁰	45 ⁹
TWO ARM REAR CABLE CRUNCH	(HOLD CONTR. 5 COUNT X 10)	1) 30	2) 30		

SLIGHT SORENESS IN FR. DELT DURING P.B.N. ; GOOD SQUEEZES   FELT REAR DELT REAL WELL
         GREAT DOWN RACKS!

WOKE UP EARLY THIS A.M.   WAS DREAMING A LOT LAST NIGHT . MOTIVATION
VERY HIGH FOR NIGHT OF CHAMP.   FRONT THIGH AND HAMSTRINGS REAL SORE
    LOTS OF WORK AROUND HOUSE TODAY   MUCH STRESS FROM TELEPHONE
BUSINESS — MEDITATION IN AFTERNOON
     TOOK DOGS FOR LONG WALK   HOME & TO BED 11:45 PM
RAIN - NICE CLOUDS TODAY.

(TANNING BED) 30 MIN ✓

AEROBICS STATIONARY BIKE ; 30 MIN. 70%   6:30 - 7:00 PM
                                                AT HOME

Showing my hard-won V-shape to the audience.

7

THE BACK: BUILDING LATS, TRAPS AND ERECTORS

The back requires a variety of exercises because it has so many different aspects that must be developed. Areas requiring individual movements are the latissimus dorsi (middle and outer back), the trapezius (upper back hooking into the shoulder) and the erectors (lower back).

All these muscles must be attended to, keeping two things in mind:

1. You must build mass and separation into all sections of the back to give it detail and thickness.
2. You must build width into the lats by stretching them out to emphasize the V-shape. Your primary goal should be to create this V-shape illusion.

T H E   T R A P E Z I U S

Known to body-builders as *traps*, these are the muscles that appear to join the neck to the shoulders, forming the slope to the top of the deltoids. From the rear it can be seen that the traps form a large area in the center of the back.

Contrary to popular opinion, fully developed traps do not make the shoulders look narrow. It's bunched-up pectorals, wide hips and large midsections that detract from perceived shoulder width. Some of the broadest-looking athletes in body-building have huge trap development. Look at the trap development of Serge Nubret, Lee Haney, Cory Everson, Bev Francis or Arnold Schwarzenegger. Each is known for his or her shoulder width.

You should be aware of balance when selecting trap exercises. People with short necks usually need less development. Those with long necks should do plenty of trap work to "fill in" the area between the shoulders and neck.

The most direct trapezius exercise is the shrug, which can be done a variety of ways. Other movements that have a positive effect on the area include deadlifts, cleans and upright rowing. Most trap exercises also work the neck extensively. Somewhat heavy weights can be used for most trap exercises, but be sure to warm up with a light set or two before getting into high gear.

The traps are also indirectly affected by upright rows, deadlifts and holding the head up (as if looking at the wall in front of you) while performing bent-over rowing movements.

Trap Exercises

1. Barbell shrug
2. Two-dumbbell shrug
3. Upright rowing
4. Top-half deadlift/shrug
5. Shrug using Universal machine or Smith machine

Note: You should only include one or two of the above exercises in your routine at any given time. The trapezius respond well to direct stimulation.

Two-Dumbbell Shrugs (start)

Two-Dumbbell Shrugs (finish)

THE LATISSIMUS DORSI

The *lats* are a muscle group that must be developed in both thickness and width. Full lat development produces the illusion of a great V-shape, creating an inverted triangle from the shoulders to the hips.

The lats can be seen from both the front and the back. They are the biggest of all the back muscles and are most dramatically displayed when they're spread by stretching out the scapula (shoulder blades) on either side of the upper back.

If I had a choice of only two exercises to do for my back, I would perform wide-grip pull-ups and barbell rows. Pull-ups have more of an effect on the lats than do lat-machine pulldowns, even though on the surface the two exercises appear identical. One reason, of course, is that when doing pull-ups you start with substantial resistance: your body weight. The second reason is that you can never rest or even partially relax your grip on the bar. Once you start a set of pull-ups, you're in it 100 percent until the set is completed.

The third reason pull-ups are more result-producing, and certainly more exhausting, is that the dynamics of the movement dictate that you pull up against an absolute vertical resistance. In the lat-machine pulldown exercise you can (even subconsciously) make subtle changes in the angle at which you pull the bar downwards. This will have the effect of increasing your comfort level.

When I perform pull-ups I like to take a fairly wide grip. (When my upper arms are parallel to the floor, my hands are out a bit farther.) I'll usually pull to the front (the bar being close to the front of my face). Occasionally, I'll pull up to the back of my neck for variety. At all times the elbows must be kept back, the rib cage up. Anytime you flatten out your rib cage you're losing the effect. If you bow your back . . . you lose out.

Whenever I perform pull-ups, I cross my feet and fold my legs under my body. A good way to signal your training partner to spot you is to simply uncross your feet. It's a good visual signal and will save your having to give verbal directions that can alter breathing patterns and break concentration.

The primary function of the wide-grip pull-up is to stretch out the scapula so that their natural position is set wider than normal.

Rowing movements are the key for back thickness. You should always keep in mind that there are multiple layers within a body part.

You have to pay attention to them all. This is especially important with back development, which affects the area all the way from the neck to the butt. Rowing in the bent-over position has been criticized by some because of the lower back injuries that have resulted. The way to avoid injury is to work from a solid base. Keep your position solid: feet flat, back flat, head up, knees bent. Do not use excessive weights. The contraction and feel is what we're after. I use bent-over row exercises frequently because I believe they're superior exercises for thickness. I've never suffered any injury as the result of using them.

Caution: When using movements in a bent-over position, use weights that allow perfect exercise form.

Lat Exercises

1. Wide-grip pull-ups to front

2. Wide-grip pull-ups to rear

3. Bent-over barbell rowing

4. Two-dumbbell rowing

5. T-bar rowing

6. Wide-grip lat pulldowns to front

7. Wide-grip lat pulldowns to rear

8. Seated low pulley row

9. One-dumbbell row

10. Close-grip pulldown

Wide-Grip Pull-ups to Front

T-Bar Rowing

Wide-Grip Lat Pulldowns to Front

Seated Low Pulley Row

Close-Grip Pulldown

THE LOWER BACK

The region of the lower back (known as the lumbar region or the erectors) should not be neglected. Its strength is a definite health benefit, and well-developed erectors certainly help give the physique that finished look.

Although the deadlift strongly affects this region, the ultimate exercise for the lower back is the prone hyperextension. Unlike the deadlift there's very little chance of incurring injury with this movement; in fact, it's frequently recommended for certain low-back sufferers. I do, however, believe in using an exercise variation of the deadlift. I call this the top-half deadlift. You assume the normal deadlifting position, but only take the bar down to just below the knees, in a very controlled way. As you raise up to the top of the lift, you squeeze the lower back. I also sometimes perform a shrug at the top of the half-deadlift movement, thereby creating a total trapezius-erector exercise.

Years ago, when body-building was still to some extent an offshoot of Olympic lifting, many lifters believed in performing heavy cleans (raising the bar from the floor to the shoulders) for ultimate back development. Certainly, many athletes of the era possessed heavily muscled backs, but they were still lifters' backs and not the more balanced and detailed backs of today's body-builders.

In my case I've found that heavy cleans are a jarring exercise. They can really mess with your tendons. I never feel comfortable performing them. I would suggest including them in your armory of exercises only if you have no lower back or shoulder-joint problems, since they're one of the most ballistic movements in weight training.

Lower Back Exercises

1. Prone hyperextension
2. Good-morning exercise (bow performed with barbell across back of shoulders)
3. Regular deadlift
4. Half deadlift
5. Stiff-leg deadlift

__Half Deadlift__

As I suggested previously, your back workout should consist of at least one exercise for each of the four different aspects: lat width, lat thickness, the traps and the erectors. Here are a few exercise combinations that I include in my armory of back routines. Remember, use your exercise armory, your journal and the principles of balance and variety to create new routines of your own.

Back Routines 1

1. Wide-grip pull-ups behind neck
2. T-bar rows
3. Barbell shrugs
4. Prone hyperextensions

Back Routines 2

1. Wide-grip lat pulldowns to front
2. Bent-over barbell row
3. Seated close-grip low pulley
4. Two-dumbbell shrugs
5. Half deadlift/shrug

As I suggested earlier, one of the most effective exercises for back development is the wide-grip pull-up, because it isolates the scapula and "pulls out" the winglike lat muscles. Another way to pull out the lats is to practice the lat-spread pose. Place your hands just above the hipbone. Push inwards and backwards so that the lat muscles flare out to the side. It may not happen the first time, but practice makes perfect.

Back Routines 3

1. Wide-grip pull-ups to front (elbows back)
2. One-dumbbell row
3. Close-grip pulldown
4. Low pulley row
5. Half deadlift/shrug

Back Routines 4

1. Wide-grip pulldown to rear
2. Two-dumbbell row
3. T-bar row
4. Barbell shrugs
5. Prone hyperextensions

MY PERSONAL ARMORY OF BACK EXERCISES

Pull-ups to front

Pull-ups to rear

Front pulldown

Rear pulldown

Close-grip pulldown

Low pulley row

One-dumbbell row

Barbell row

T-bar row

Straight pulling

Two-dumbbell row

Traps

Barbell shrug

Dumbbell shrug

Half deadlift/shrug

Lower Back

Stiff-leg deadlift

Hyperextension

Good mornings

8

THE CHEST: BALANCING THE PECTORALS

Everyone wants to build an impressive chest. It's an acknowledged hallmark of physical perfection.

But care must be taken when building the chest because it's easy to take an unbalanced approach. Too many body-builders rely just on the basic bench press for their chest development. The danger in excessive benching is that the pecs could eventually appear too bunched up or too developed in the lower areas. And while we're on the subject, does every chest workout have to start with the bench press? What's the logic behind this? Why has starting a workout with this exercise become a ritual with nearly all body-builders? Perhaps because the bench press has become an ego exercise. Some men take great pleasure in starting a workout with three forty-five-pound plates on each end of the bar. But it's a waste—you should *feel* the contraction with the bench press, just as you should with all resistance exercises. Don't mistake me: I'm not against the bench press—it's great. It works ... but why must it always be the first chest exercise we perform? Would anyone dare *end* a workout with bench presses? In some gyms this would be regarded as almost blasphemous.

Whether you're a competitive body-builder or not, the chest

muscles should be built proportionately. That is to say, the upper-outer areas should get a lot of work. The reason behind this is that whether they're viewed under an overhead series of lights (as you'd find in a contest setting) or under bright sun, pectorals that are built high and toward the outer reaches are far more likely to make a physique appear outstanding than those built from the performance of *randomly* selected chest exercises. I am not saying that you shouldn't build the lower pecs or the inner pecs. These areas must be exercised to give them a degree of mass and hardness, but the major emphasis should be on the upper and outer areas. The development of the outer curve of the pecs makes the whole chest and shoulder area look wider, more visually flared, much more impressive.

At my seminars I'm often asked if the rib cage can be enlarged with exercise. The answer is yes, but only marginally. You can't *completely* change your chest structure from a flat-type rib cage to a Lou Ferrigno barrel-type variation. What *is* possible to achieve is increased rib-cage depth (thickness). An inch or possibly two in rib-cage expansion is not out of the question, but it could take a year or more of proper exercises to bring it about.

R I B - C A G E E X P A N S I O N P R O G R A M

Twice a week perform the following routine either on your "off days" or at the end of your leg-training program.

Superset	Sets	Reps
Back squat	3	25–30
Across-bench dumbbell pullover	3	15–25

Across-Bench Dumbbell Pullover (start)

Across-Bench Dumbbell Pullover

It's important that you transition right from the squat exercise to the pullover without any rest. Start the pullover well before your heavy breathing (induced by the squatting) has returned to normal. Use a medium weight for the squats; no resting between repetitions. Use a moderate weight for the pullovers that will enable you to perform fifteen to twenty-five reps. The object is to stretch the rib cage each time the dumbbell is lowered behind the head. Take one deep breath with each repetition of squats and one deep breath between each repetition of pullovers. As the dumbbell lowers to almost touch the ground, the lungs should be full of air. Pause for a "one thousand and one" count—raise and repeat.

Frank Zane increased his rib-cage capacity with lots of lung-bursting leg work combined with across-bench dumbbell pullovers. This gave him one of the most dramatic and physically beautiful rib cages in bodybuilding. Frank always ended his posing routine by displaying his rib-cage vacuum, his favorite pose. It brought the house down.

I think that my term *intelligent mass building* applies to the chest as much as it does any body part. How many unattractive, bunched-up,

Parallel Bar Dips
(emphasis on pectorals)

rounded pectorals have you seen lately? Chest exercises come in two distinct categories: There are exercises that draw the arms across the body from the side. And there are exercises that push resistance away from the body. To build intelligent mass you should build into your routine exercises from both categories.

Many people are fascinated by pectoral striations. There is, unfortunately, no single movement that brings these out; striations are the result of variety training and a calorie-controlled diet. It not only helps to work hard but also to have thin skin.

I'm frequently asked about dipping exercises (on the parallel bar stand). People want to know if the exercise is a triceps movement or a chest movement. This is one exercise, when performed on a standard set of dip stands, that really works two distinctly different body parts extremely efficiently. More emphasis can be put on the pectorals, though, if the chin is pressed down into the chest and the feet are held in front (forward) of the body. Make a concave (curved inward) shape with the body and keep the elbows out to the sides. Now, this exercise really works the chest, but more important, it puts the stress on the most neglected part of the pectorals, the outside area so important for that wide upper-body appearance.

One muscle group that contributes to the chest and torso completeness is the serratus. This is the *shark's tooth muscle* that appears to join the lats to the torso by inserting into the ribs. When you're carrying low body fat this muscle will show up impressively on both sides of the chest. People unfamiliar with anatomy often mistake the serratus muscle for the ribs.

There's no single exercise that totally isolates the serratus, but movements such as across-bench pullovers, Nautilus pullovers, flat and incline flyes, pull-ups and pulldowns, overhead pressing and pec-deck flyes have a spillover effect on the serratus. One of my favorite serratus exercises is the *top* of a lat pulldown movement, flexing the lats forward. When you're in the completely stretched position, with your arms straight above your head, push the arms and shoulders forward, flexing the lats and serratus together. Do this at the top of each rep to bring the serratus into action throughout the set. The best pose to show off (and isolate) this area is the rib-cage isolation movement with the hands behind the head, similar to the *abdominal and thigh position* in the compulsory poses, but without crunching down with the abs. This is the same pose I mentioned Zane using to show off his rib cage. It displayed his amazing serratus, too.

The following routines are drawn from my armory of exercises. You should try to create your routines from exercises that work all angles and aspects of the muscle. Include as many different angles as possible in each routine.

Create variety from workout to workout.

CHEST ROUTINES

	Sets	Reps
Workout 1		
Incline barbell press	4	8–15
Dips (for chest)	4	12–15
Incline flyes	4	8–10
Across-bench pullover	4	15–20
Workout 2		
Flat barbell press	5	6–8
Incline dumbbell press	5	10–15
Low-incline flyes	5	15–20
Workout 3		
Flat flyes	4	6–8
Dips for chest	4	12–15
Cable crossovers	4	15–20
Incline barbell press to neck	4	8–10
Workout 4		
Flat barbell press to neck	4	15–20
Low-incline flyes	4	8–10
Incline dumbbell press	3	12–15
Cable crossovers	3	20–25

A word about the cable-crossover machine. This can be a very useful tool because, depending on how you perform the exercise, you can build any part of the pectoral muscle you wish. The cable-crossover machine is extremely versatile. Stand forward of the machine and you will work the outer pecs; stand back slightly of the two uprights, cross your hands over at the conclusion of each rep and you'll stress the central part of the chest. Additionally, you can work the upper areas by holding the hands at chin level or the lower section by keeping the hands at waist level.

Cable Crossover (start)

Cable Crossover (finish)

Anyone can improve his chest appearance. The secret is balance. Once you determine what areas of your chest need the most work, you can tailor your routine accordingly. But you won't notice the emergence of a new chest shape immediately. It takes time. In any case, don't revert back to the standard *flat benches and flyes* if you really know that your chest needs wide-grip dips and incline dumbbell presses . . . check your requirements, select your exercises and stick with the exercises you know will help you look more impressive.

You may have noticed that several body-builders on the pro circuit have torn or otherwise injured their pecs.

It seems that the pecs, because they often have extremely heavy demands put on them via heavy bench presses and flye movements, are prone to injury. This is especially true when a body-builder is trying to bring his or her body-fat levels down in order to rip up. Fat helps cushion and protect a muscle, and when there's no fat in the area an injury can occur. A torn pec can be operated on with 100 percent success, but the operation has to be done immediately. It's far better, of course, never to have an injury. You can take steps to avoid needless tears by warming up with one or two moderate sets before loading up the barbell to your limit poundage. Above all, preserve good mind-muscle control. No ballistic movements, no bouncing, no jerking. Keep your pectoral exercises smooth, controlled and in the groove, and you should never experience an injured pec . . .ever!

MY PERSONAL ARMORY OF CHEST EXERCISES

Bench press

Incline bench press

Incline dumbbell bench press

Flat flye

Incline flye

Pec-deck

Cable crossover

Cable crossover on incline bench

Dips

Bench press to neck

Push-ups

Flat dumbbell bench press

Across-bench pullover

• • • • •

9

THE LEGS: MOLDING SUPER QUADS, CALVES AND HAMSTRINGS

• • • • •

When it comes to thigh training, there are two distinct areas that require development—the front thigh and the hamstring (though each, of course, is divided into more segmented muscles). You need to find a balance of strength between the two. A lot of knee problems result from an imbalance of strength: an incredible amount of strength in the front thigh and a lack of strength in the hamstring. The old school of thought was that by doing squats for the thighs, you were also working the hamstrings sufficiently. It's my feeling, though, that the hamstrings should be worked directly in a two-to-three ratio with the front thighs (e.g., ten sets for the hamstrings, fifteen sets for the front thighs). Now, that's not cast in stone; it also depends on your current strength and weakness in both those muscles. The goal, of course, is evenly developed muscle from knee to hip and from the back of the knee up to the buttocks (glutes).

Leg development definitely has to be planned—otherwise too many things can go wrong. If you have skinny quads, then squats have to form a basic part of your leg workouts. You should be aware, though, that excessive squatting, especially when combined with a very high-calorie diet, can lead to glutes that are too big or "spread."

Individuals who have long femurs (thighbones) will find that regular squats don't give them the overall upper leg development they need. When these people squat, the major part of the stress is placed on the upper thighs and hips and only a small percentage is on the middle and lower thigh. The problem can be "beaten" to a certain extent by placing a block of wood (two-and-one-half inches thick) under the heels during the exercise. This enables the person to squat with the back more erect (vertical) and, accordingly, places more of the stress lower down the thigh. This more upright stance also takes some stress away from the glutes.

Those with relatively "short" thighs will find that no block of wood is required under the heels. A flat-footed squat (using normal exercise footwear) will affect the lower, middle and upper thigh areas equally.

Even so, body-builders can't rely solely on the squat to build the legs. True, the squat involves some hamstring action, some calf involvement, some sartorius, etc., but legs need more variety to pull them into *real* shape. I'm not saying you have to perform every leg muscle in the book, but legs must be balanced if you want them to be impressive.

What does an impressive, balanced leg look like? The thighs should have an outer curve that begins at the hipbone and continues to sweep dramatically, until tucking in at the knee joint. The upper thighs should have distinct separation between the muscles. The sartorius should be able to be seen clearly on the inside of the leg. Hamstrings should bulge so that there is an attractive back-leg curve to balance the frontal thigh mass. Knees and ankles should be bony and entirely fat free. Calves should hold a balance between the development on the outside and the inside. Not only should they appear *diamond-shaped* from the front, but the division between the two gastrocnemius heads when viewed from the back should be clear and sharp, at least when one calf is flexed. Additionally, calves and thighs should appear thick from the side view, as well as balanced from the frontal positions.

It may seem obvious to advise that the legs be trained for balanced development, but very few actually adopt this approach. Of course, what you should do is train hardest, and concentrate most, on those areas that lack development. The following information will help you structure your leg routine. Naturally, it's hardly possible, or even advisable, to perform all the leg exercises that I'm listing. Simply select one or two exercises for the lower legs and three or four exercises for the upper legs. And switch them around regularly.

Upper Leg Exercises

Lunges (upper thigh rods)

Regular back squat (upper and middle thigh)

Back squat, heels on block (mid and lower thigh)

Hack squat (mid and lower thigh)

Forty-five-degree leg presses (overall quad development)

Lying (vertical) leg press (lower and middle thigh)

Leg extension (mid- and low-thigh separation)

Leg extension, lying flat on back (upper and middle thigh)

Standing leg curl (middle hamstring)

Stiff-leg deadlifts (middle hamstring)

Lying leg curl (lower and mIddle hamstring)

Sissy squats (lower and middle thigh)

Leg squeeze with pulleys (inner thigh)

Hack Squat

Going for the burn on the leg-extension machine.

Standing Leg Curl

Lower Leg Exercises

Standing calf raise (overall gastrocnemius)

Seated calf raise (soleus)

Calf raise on leg-press machine (lower gastrocnemius)

Donkey calf raise (overall gastrocnemius)

To perform the overall gastrocnemius, stand on a high block. Bend forward, resting your upper body on a medium-height bar or piece of equipment (such as the edge of a leg-curl machine). Have a training partner climb onto your back just above where your hips are bent so that it looks as if he or she is "riding a donkey." Using the partner's weight as your resistance, raise your calves to their maximum contraction and lower to their maximum stretch (see chapter 13, "Buddy Training," for illustration).

Many people write asking me to itemize exactly what exercises they should perform for their legs. They tell me, "Map me out an exact routine and I'll follow it to the letter." They even want me to detail the exact sets and reps. This, of course, is impossible to do with any degree of accuracy, because I don't know all the variables. Even if these individuals sent me photos showing their legs from a variety of angles, I'd still be in the dark about their eating habits, health, medical history, tolerance for strenuous physical exercise, motivation levels and a score of other factors. Still, having said that, I'm going to list some typical (workable) leg routines that have proven successful for athletes from all parts of the country. Bear in mind that your leg routine is only about one third or one quarter of your entire training schedule. It has to mesh with your overall training routine. Don't fall into the trap of selecting too many exercises. You could burn yourself out. The following are a few good leg routines that I personally recommend:

	Sets	Reps
Routine 1		
Back squat	4	8
Hack squat	4	10–12
Lying leg press	4	15
Dumbbell leg curl	4	12–15
Standing leg curl	4	12–15
Standing calf raise	4	12–15
Seated calf raise	4	15–20
Routine 2		
Front squat	4	12
Forty-five-degree leg presses	4	12–15
Lying leg curl	4	12–15
Stiff-leg deadlift	4	15
Leg-press toe raise	4	20–25
Donkey raise	4	20–25
Routine 3		
Leg press	4	25
Lunges	4	15–20
Ballet squat	4	25–30
Standing leg curl	4	15–20
Lying leg curl	4	15–20
Standing calf raise	4	25–30
Tibia raise[a]	4	20–25
Seated calf raise	4	20–25

	Sets	Reps
Routine 4		
Back squat	3	35–40
Leg extension	4	12–15
Lying leg press	4	15
Standing leg curl	4	12–15
Stiff-leg deadlift	4	15–20
Leg-press calf raise	4	25–30
Standing calf raise	4	25–30

a A description of the tibia-raise exercise follows in text.

The tibia raise develops the muscles around the shin. Stand on a high block. Your heels should be on the block and the front of your feet forward of it. Stretch your toes toward the ground, pivoting on your heels, for the bottom of the movement. Then raise them as high as possible, fully contracting the muscle of the front of the calf. This exercise will create balanced development in your calves by building an often neglected area.

The calves are high-rep muscle. Don't perform less than twelve reps for any calf exercise. Squats do build the calves, but never to the same degree that they build the upper legs. You should never miss training the calves. If you're genetically endowed with either high or low calves, there is not too much you can do to change their basic shape. For example, a high calf can be stretched by lowering the heels down as far as humanly possible between each repetition, but, sadly, only minimal lengthening will take place. You can't "pull down" a high calf.

It's generally recognized that when you do calf raises with the toes pointing inward, the outer part of the calf muscle is worked; point the toes outward and the inside (diamond) area is trained. If you don't lack in either inner or outer leg development, then perform your calf raises with the feet facing straight forward.

In all body-part training I like to work with a wide variety of repetitions—nowhere is this more true than with leg exercises. My reps can range anywhere from six to fifty. When training legs I consider twenty to twenty-five to be medium repetitions; high reps are in the range of thirty-five to fifty. I've seen body-builders who have sticking points with their thighs make incredible improvement doing higher-repetition exercises, especially if they get stuck in the groove of doing low-rep squats.

I believe it's vital to flex the muscle you're training when you work the legs. Let's take the leg press as an example. There are three different ways to do a leg press:

1. *The regular leg press.* Simply move the weight up and down in a normal fashion. With feet flat against the board, power the resistance up and down, giving no thought to feeling the contraction or flexing the thighs.

2. *Involving the hamstrings.* Perform the bottom of the movement only; press the weight up to about three quarters of the way up, flexing the hamstrings and continuing a nonstop up-down rhythm—no locking out at all.

3. *Muscle-flexing press.* The best technique for bringing out the separation in the front thigh, especially in the lower front thigh, is to raise the toes off the platform, pressing with the heel as the weight resistance reaches the top point. As you get to the top, flex the front thighs. (The act of raising the toes off the board does not in itself flex the thigh; it merely puts the thigh in a better position to flex.) When you flex you're putting all your power into the core of the muscle, ripping as many fibers as possible.

Leg training is tough. You hate to do it and yet you hate not to do it. I never cease to be amazed at how many fitness buffs and body-builders do no leg training at all! This should *never* happen. Even if you have natural leg development, you should still train your legs vigorously twice a week. It's good for your heart, your circulatory system, your metabolism—and besides, a leg that isn't weight-trained lacks that special look that spells true fitness, health and strength.

MY PERSONAL ARMORY OF LEG EXERCISES

Front Thigh

Back squat

Front squat

Hack squat

Sissy squat

Forty-five-degree leg presses

Lying leg press

Lunges

Ballet squat

Leg extensions

Hamstrings

Lying leg curl

Standing leg curl

Dumbbell leg curl

Calves

Standing calf raise

Seated calf raise

Leg-press calf raise

Donkey calf raise

Tibia lifts

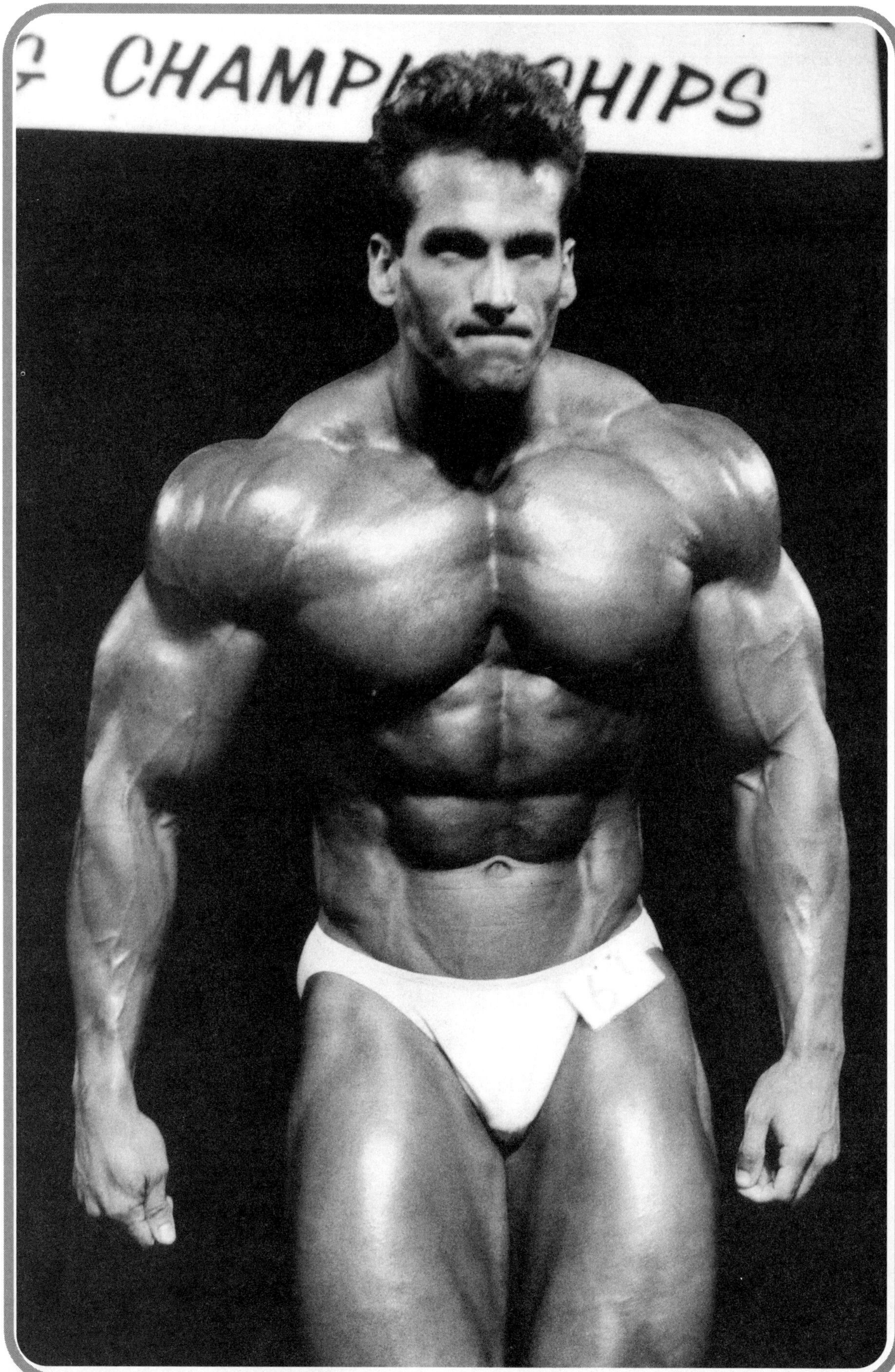
CHAMPI
HIPS

10

THE SHOULDERS: THREE-SIDED DELTOID DEVELOPMENT

Every upper body exercise you do works the shoulders in some way. Think about it . . . bench presses, pulldowns, curls, dips. . . . The shoulders get an enormous amount of spillover stress. For this reason it's possible, because of this accessory work, to overtrain the deltoids.

The shoulders serve a couple of different functions:

1. To press objects (weights) away from the body.
2. To laterally raise and rotate the arms.

Consequently, you need to employ the exercises that utilize these actions. Basically, the shoulder muscles have three aspects: the front, the side and the back. Because most body-builders tend to perform plenty of incline and flat bench movements, the front deltoid often has pretty good development. Even so, I think that some specialized front deltoid exercises should be incorporated into your shoulder routine.

Remember my key word: *variety*. It applies especially to the deltoid, because it's a three-headed muscle. Certainly, no shoulder

Universal Machine Military Press

routine can be described as complete unless it contains a minimum of three exercises, one for each deltoid head. No single exercise works all three heads adequately. So, for example, if you're an intermediate performing eight sets for your shoulders, it would make much more sense to train using two sets of four different exercises, rather than four sets of two different exercises.

Can the width of the clavicles (natural bone width) be changed with exercise? More widening is likely with years of performing exercises like wide-grip pull-ups (rather than pressing movements), but even so, any increase in bone width would be measured in tenths of inches rather than inches. It is comforting to note that whereas height tends to level out at around eighteen or nineteen years of age, the natural widening of the shoulders can continue into the midtwenties or even later.

I've seen some people working the deltoids with several sets of heavy movements, only to conclude their shoulder routine with a couple of sets of what they call "pumping reps." I don't believe this to be an effective way to train the delts or any other muscle group. My philosophy remains the same regardless of body part: you must rotate your movements frequently (drawing on your armory of preselected exercises); select a variety of rep patterns, but not fewer than six; and concentrate on *feeling* the contraction, squeezing it and holding it for a beat, before continuing on. . . . By all means, take your deltoid training into the range of twenty to twenty-five reps, but don't regard these sets as merely pumping sets. Perform these high reps *slowly*, with conviction and concentration, and above all take them to positive failure. It's really important to find the contraction—you have to *earn the right* to move on to the next rep by doing the previous one faultlessly.

For those men and women who seek a balanced body, good deltoid development is important. As I said before, all three heads should be attacked. Whereas the most obvious head to train is the side head, because it adds impressive width to the body, it's also imperative that plenty of isolation work be devoted to the rear area. Without sufficient rear deltoid development the back will lack detail and you will appear round-shouldered.

FRONT DELTOID

When this head is built to the max it will add a ravine between the front delt and the upper pectoral—a new detail to catch the stage light and the judges' eye.

Maximum frontal deltoid development is vital to the competitive body-builder when the double-biceps-from-the-rear pose is performed. The height of the deltoids in this position depends *entirely* on the degree of development of the front deltoid section.

SIDE DELTOID

The admiration of wide shoulders has been with us for centuries. As a body-builder you'd better put in workout time to develop shoulder width. You'll need side deltoid development in almost *every* pose, and when you're compared to other competitors in the relaxed position, the side delts are *everything.*

REAR DELTOID

It used to be thought that the rear deltoid would take care of itself as the result of doing the press behind neck, pulldowns, pull-ups, dips or rows. True, some rear deltoid stimulation results from these exercises, but a rear delt isolation exercise is needed, and it should be included in every shoulder workout! You may be surprised to know that the rear deltoid plays a significant role in a competitive body-builder's quest for titles. It's one of the main attractions in the compulsory back and side poses, even in the relaxed back and side positions. The following are some suggested shoulder-building routines that I've used and some that I've not used exactly as shown, but have seen work well for others. Remember that even though I'm giving you several routines, my own philosophy is *to build a routine from an armory of preselected exercises*. My routine may vary with each workout for weeks and weeks, or, if I'm getting good results, I may stay with a certain combination for a series of consecutive workouts. But variety in repetition patterns and exercise selection remains one of my guiding principles.

The bent-over dumbbell side raise is the best
isolation exercise for the rear head of the deltoid.

	Sets	Reps
Routine 1		
Press behind neck (side and front delt)	3	8–10
Alternate forward dumbbell raise (front delts)	4	12–15
Bent-over dumbbell side raise (rear delts)	4	12–15
Side raise (side delts)	4	12–15
Routine 2		
Seated dumbbell press (side and front delts)	3	12
Upright row (front and side delts)	3	10–15
Side-raise machine (side delts)	3	15–20
Reverse pec-deck (rear delts)	3	15–20
Dumbbell front raise (front delts)	3	15
Routine 3		
Dumbbell press (side and front delts)	4	6–12
One-arm pulley side raise (side delts)	3	12–15
Low-cable front raise (front delts)	3	12–15
Two-pulley rear crunch (rear delts)	3	15–20
Routine 4		
Upright row (front and side delts)	3	10–12
Bent-over pulley side raise (front and side delts)	3	12–15
Seated dumbbell side raise (side delts)	3	12–15
Incline side raise (side delts)	3	12–15
Press behind neck (side and front delts)	3	25

One-Arm Pulley Side Raise

Blasting my front delts
with upright rows.

MY PERSONAL ARMORY OF SHOULDER EXERCISES

Press behind neck

Dumbbell press

Upright row

One-arm pulley side raise

Bent-over pulley side raise

Seated dumbbell side raise

Bent-over dumbbell side raise

Incline side raise

Lying compound side raise

Two-pulley rear crunch

Reverse pec-deck

• • • • •

11

THE ARMS: SCULPTING THE BICEPS, TRICEPS AND FOREARMS

• • • • •

Arms come in all shapes and sizes. You'll see these differences even among body-builders who train regularly. Some athletes have high biceps; others have flat biceps. You'll see triceps that run right down to the elbows in some, while others have what can only be described as high triceps. Forearms, too, can be very differently shaped. Some people have "long" wrists with most of their forearm development high, near the elbow; others are genetically inclined to have forearms that maintain thickness almost right to the wrist.

My view is that you should maximize arm development, but only in accordance with the other muscle groups of your physique. The Greek ideal that the arms (flexed), neck and calves should be of the same size still holds true, at least in my eyes. The current view of most professional body-builders, though, is that the arms should be much bigger than the neck and the calf. Some judges seem to like this "freaky" look (where one body part is disproportionate), so in a way I can't blame body-builders for jumping on the bandwagon. Nevertheless, my instinct is toward perfect symmetry, and it's what I recommend,

Feeling the pushdown.

regardless of whether you want to attain contest shape or a lighter physical impressiveness.

Just about all the exercises you perform affect the arms in one way or another. Even heavy squats will help put size on your arms. Even so, a correctly balanced physique can't be built without the use of specific arm exercises. The upper arm consists mainly of three muscles, the biceps (a two-headed muscle on top of the arm), the triceps (a three-headed muscle on the underside of the arm) and the braccialis (a hardly seen muscle in the front of the arm, located for the most part under the biceps). The lower arm consists primarily, for body-building purposes, of the forearm.

Although the forearms are worked strenuously in most exercises, developing them to their fullest is something you should attempt, and you should do it with specialized forearm exercises. Mike Mentzer used to say that he never needed to perform any specific forearm movements because he used the heavy-duty system of training (low sets and extreme effort, taken to beyond failure each set). There may be some validity to this approach, because Mike did have wonderful forearm development, but then again, there are many proponents of the heavy-duty system who *don't* have incredible forearms. If you're genetically inclined to slimness in the lower arm area, then I strongly advise a forearm blitz at least twice a week. Like the calves and abdominals, the forearms are a high-rep muscle. You'll do better utilizing a system of fifteen to twenty-five reps than using low counts of five to eight.

T R I C E P S

When training triceps it's important to feel the belly of the muscle, and not just the flexing of the elbow. Perform a pushdown and *feel* the tie-in right there. You can easily miss the feel if you're not concentrating on the movement.

Another important aspect, especially when performing the lying French press, is the stretch. As the weight is lowered, concentrate on keeping those elbows in (remember that you have an imaginary rope around the elbows to hold them in place) and feel that important stretch. I see all triceps movements as falling into one of two categories:

1. *The extension exercises:* pushdowns, overhead extensions, lying French presses, dumbbell extensions, etc.
2. *The pressing exercises:* regular dips, bench dips, close-grip bench presses, etc. (these exercises work the belly of the muscle).

A word about the close-grip bench press: if you find that your hands get sweaty (and you don't like wearing gloves), there may be a tendency

Lying French Press

for your hands to slip wider as the set gets under way. In this case you can use an EZ curl bar. The camber is ideal for this exercise and you will find your grip keeps in place throughout the set. If you incorporate the close-grip bench press into your triceps routine, then try and work your triceps on a chest day. Close-grip bench presses resemble numerous key chest exercises, and their performance prior to a chest day can interfere with the recovery process.

When you're doing triceps pressing movements, it's important to find the muscle belly by stopping just a fraction of an inch from full "lock out" in the contraction position. This way the full force of the lifted weight rests on the contracted muscle and not just on the skeletal structure.

BICEPS

Beauty is in the eye of the beholder, but there are some aspects to arm development that people agree on. For example, although changing arm shape is possible, it can only be done to a small degree. You can't pull a high triceps down, but you can put emphasis on the lower aspects of the triceps to maximize the cell enlargement in that lower triceps area.

I'm not a proponent of high, knotted, peaked biceps. I far prefer a fully developed, rotund biceps that tucks in low down the arm (near the elbow) and rises to a well-rounded, but not peaked, crest when the arms are flexed. But as I've said, changes in arm shape can be made on a limited basis. It's a matter of sticking with the principle of employing a variety of rep patterns and making each selected exercise work the area of the arm you want to build. For example, preacher curls, with barbells or dumbbells, tend to work the lower biceps area and fill in the gap at the crook of the arm. When you direct your mind-muscle concentration into the lower biceps, thinking the stress into the lower biceps as you begin to curl, more improvements can be expected. But don't expect a dramatic change in shape. It never happens. The same goes for those who desire more roundness to their biceps. You can employ a system of isolating the biceps by using concentration curls, either with a dumbbell or pulley. Take the resistance through its complete range of motion, feeling the contraction, squeezing it all the way so that the biceps are momentarily cramped, and there will be improvement, worthwhile improvement. But as for a complete alteration of shape, that's unlikely. Remember that in body-building you can take steps to improve the balance of *any* area by utilizing two practices:

1. Working and placing the mental direction in the area you want to build.
2. Not working the area you want to reduce.

Dumbbell Kickback (start)

Dumbbell Kickback (finish)

If, for example, you have a high triceps (all your development is near the shoulders), you can attack the problem on two fronts. First, you can perform lower triceps exercises, like dumbbell kickbacks or overhead triceps extensions, and at the same time you might cut back on movements like the lying triceps extension that could put too much emphasis on the triceps near the shoulder. Once you've corrected the balance, return again to selecting a wide variety of movements from your armory of arm exercises.

I try as much as possible to remain true to my system of variety—though, to be honest, I frequently find myself starting my triceps exercises with some variation of the pushdown. However, I don't think it would be a good idea, especially if you're heavy, to begin your triceps working with dips using your entire body weight. Your ligaments and joints may not be fully warmed up, and injury could occur.

How many arm exercises should you include in your workouts? Absolute beginners should perform only one biceps and one triceps exercise. Intermediates can use two or three exercises for each muscle group, and advanced trainers can use three or four exercises each for triceps, biceps and forearms (a total of nine to twelve different exercises for the entire arm workout).

The following are several arm routines that have proved effective for me over the years.

TRICEPS ROUTINES

	Sets	Reps
Routine 1		
Lying French press	4	6–8
Bench dips	4	12–15
Two-dumbbell kickbacks	4	15–20
Routine 2		
Pushdown (straight bar)	4	8–10
Overhead pulley extension	4	10–12
Dips for triceps	3–4	15–20
Routine 3		
Close-grip bench press	4	15–20
Dips	4	12–15
One-arm dumbbell triceps extension	4	12–15

	Sets	Reps
Routine 4		
Pushdown (V-bar)	4	8–12
Incline triceps extension	4	12–15
Lying one-dumbbell extension	4	15–20

Overhead Pulley Extension (start)

Overhead Pulley Extension (finish)

BICEPS ROUTINES

	Sets	Reps
Routine 1		
Incline dumbbell curl	4	6–8
Barbell curl	4	10–15
Seated concentration curl	4	15–20
Routine 2		
Standing dumbbell curl	4	8–10
Barbell preacher curl	4	10–12
Incline dumbbell curl	3–4	15–20
Routine 3		
Seated alternate dumbbell curl	3	15–20
One-dumbbell preacher curl	3	6–8
Barbell curl	3	20–25
One-arm pulley curl	3	10–12
Routine 4		
Barbell curl	4	6–8
Barbell preacher curl	4	6–8
Alternate dumbbell curl	4	8–10

__Dumbbell__ __Curls__

__Barbell__ __Curls__

I've also included here a sticking-point workout for biceps and triceps that you may like to try out if your upper arms are refusing to grow. Remember when tri-setting for a body part that you must perform the individual exercise so that you find each contraction on *every* rep. Move in a cycle from one exercise to the next.

		Sets	Reps
Biceps			
Tri-Set	Incline dumbbell curl	3–4	12–10
	Close grip barbell curl EZ bar	3–4	12–20
	Pulley two-arm preacher curl	3–4	12–20
Triceps			
Tri-Set	Pushdown	3–4	12–20
	Bench dips	3–4	12–20
	Two-dumbbell kickbacks	3–4	12–20

Bench Dips

The forearms are worked anytime you hold a dumbbell or barbell, but there's still a need for specialized training twice a week. Reps for lower arm training should be in the twelve-to-twenty-five range. When I perform the wrist curl I use a *false* grip (thumbs under the bar), but this is because I have a bad wrist problem, not because I think a false grip gives the forearms a better workout. I do make a point of lowering the weight as far down as I can, but I don't roll it out on the fingers. One of my favorite forearm supersets involves using a low cable with a short, rotating bar. Sitting on the floor, I perform wrist curls first, and then, changing the weight downwards, follow quickly with a set of reverse wrist curls (overhand grip). I keep alternating these two exercises until my forearms are exhausted.

The following are examples of specialized forearm routines:

FOREARMS

	Sets	Reps
Routine 1		
Standing barbell reverse curl	4	12–20
Seated wrist curl	4	12–20
Routine 2		
Zottman curl (palms facing each other)	3	12–15
Low-cable wrist curl	3	15–25
Low-cable reverse wrist curl	3	15–25
Routine 3		
Seated barbell wrist curl	5	12–15
Reverse barbell preacher curl	5	15–20

Note: The wrist and elbow joints, both of which can be involved maximally in arm training, can be subject to injury if you make a practice of performing single or excessively low repetitions. Always warm up well with moderate weights before taking your arm training to maximum effort.

Not only should your arms be built in proportion to your torso, back and legs, but the individual arm areas should balance with each other. Large upper arms need good forearm development to maintain overall harmony. Similarly, the biceps shouldn't overshadow the triceps or vice versa. There must be a reason for every rep you perform, and that all-important reason is balance.

Seated Barbell Wrist Curl

Standing Barbell
Reverse Curl

Zottman Curl
(also called a
Hammer Curl)

MY PERSONAL ARMORY OF ARM EXERCISES

Biceps

Barbell curl

Barbell preacher curl

Two-arm pulley preacher curl

Two-arm pulley curl

Incline dumbbell curl

Seated alternate curl

Concentration curl

One-pulley curl

One-dumbbell preacher curl

Triceps

Pushdown

Reverse pushdown

Rope pushdowns

One-dumbbell extension

Lying French press

Barbell kickback

Two-dumbbell kickback

Two-arm one-dumbbell extension

Bench dips

Overhead pulley

Seated French press

One-arm pushdown

One-arm extension

Forearms

Barbell wrist curl

Dumbbell wrist curl

Reverse curl

Zottman curl

Cable reverse curl

Cable reverse wrist curl

12

THE ABDOMINALS: MUSCLING UP THE MIDSECTION

We all want a slim waistline; yet such a condition eludes literally tens of millions of North Americans. Abdominal exercises are important. The waist needs to be kept strong and tight, but the most important factor is diet control. You should eat wholesome foods, and you should control your calorie intake to the point where superfluous fat is burned up. People usually groan when I tell them that they have to eat properly, but I respond by saying that it's just as easy to eat a balanced, healthy diet as it is to eat junk food. Heck, you'll even save money; good food invariably costs less than junk food.

The midsection is made up of a wall of muscle between the sternum and the pelvis. There are also intercostal muscles that mobilize the torso when it's turned. The action of the main abdominal wall is to draw the pelvis and sternum closer together.

In the early days of body-building the regular sit-up was King. Today, no one in his right mind performs a regular sit-up. Not only is it out of style—it doesn't work!

There has been an ongoing controversy over how many reps are best for abdominal conditioning. No one is going to deny that all variations of reps work to some degree. The abs will be worked whether you do hundreds of reps or whether you just perform one or two. The question is, of course: Which system of reps is best?

Zabo Kozewski, Ed Guiliani, Bill Pearl, Tom Platz and Frank Zane all built fabulous abs using very high repetitions. Often, these guys wouldn't count abs; they would work their abs by the clock—forty minutes, fifty minutes, sixty minutes. . . . Zabo, for example, would perform forty minutes of leg raises followed by forty minutes of roman chair sit-ups. There are a few body-builders who train their abs the same as any other body part . . . by performing eight to twelve reps only. There have even been body-builders who *never* trained abs. Reportedly, Steve Reeves was one of these. His logic was that midsection training only served to thicken the waist area.

My own belief is that the abs are a high-rep muscle (i.e., they react best to high repetitions), but I don't see the point in going much higher than twenty-five to forty reps per set.

Admittedly, the waistline gets larger as you gain weight; it's only natural. You must, however, guard against the waistline getting out of control as you add body weight. If you find this difficult, consider incorporating the following into your program:

1. Eat enough extra calories to gain muscular body weight, but *not* so many that you add fat deposits to your midsection.
2. Perform a variety of exercises for the abdominals every other day. Include light twisting exercises as well as a variety of crunches and leg raises.
3. Maintain good posture while sitting and standing. Practice partially "holding in" stomach. Soon it will become second nature.
4. Keep some form of aerobic activity in your program, such as the stair machine or stationary cycling. It will keep your metabolism hyped.

I believe the mind plays an important part in all body-building endeavors, but it has particular relevance when you're talking about abdominals.

People used to joke about Arnold Schwarzenegger's ability to concentrate during his exercises. They'd say that if he were in the middle of a set and a bomb went off in the gym, he wouldn't hear it.

Scientific studies have shown that individuals can't consciously hold concentration for more than a few seconds, but you can at least *attempt* 100 percent concentration. With practice you'll become pretty good at it. To merely concentrate on reaching your target number of repetitions is not enough—in fact, it's the wrong approach. You must make the abdominals *feel* the exercise maximally. To merely aim to complete a certain number of reps is defeating the purpose. Start a particular set of crunches or frog kicks by consciously squeezing the abs at the completion of each repetition. Don't allow your mind to stray from this action of squeezing.

Of all the body parts, abdominals seem to be the most neglected. One reason may be the rumor that too much midsection work can throw a no-gains switch on your general ability to gain mass. There's some truth to this, because excessive ab training, when you're not used to it, can excite the central nervous system and hold back overall gains. But there should be no problem if you *gradually* increase the duration and severity of your abdominal program. Bill Pearl, a multi–Mr. Universe winner, always started his workouts with forty minutes of strenuous nonstop abdominal training, and it certainly didn't keep him from gaining muscle size.

Another reason why the abs seem to get short shrift is because midsection training tends to be boring. You're not curling huge weights or pushing up mammoth poundages as in the bench press, or lifting impressive dumbbells overhead. For the most part, you're repeatedly bringing the knees into the tummy or curling the torso to the pelvis. *Boring*!

So what can you do? You have to fire up your mind to beat the bugaboo of undermotivation. You must work to create an artificial enthusiasm, until it becomes a natural, *aggressive* enthusiasm. When you begin to show results, believe me, you'll be motivated. Your inspiration and appetite for more of the same will be whetted beyond belief. Body-builders are always enormously motivated by progress. When it comes, they want more. No exercise is boring when it's obviously working.

On the other hand, some individuals may be plagued by over-enthusiasm. This too can be a huge burden. When results come too slowly, or appear not to come at all, then overenthusiasm can change to disappointment and frustration. This in turn can lead to giving up altogether. You may train too hard, too frequently and for too long, and consequently throw yourself into a sticking point. Muscles can only take so much shock treatment, and the abdominals are a sensitive area that can be overtrained. The answer is to harness your accelerating enthusiasm, to slow down the pace and decide to make progress slowly.

Men and women are often in the habit of leaving abdominal training until the end of their routines. There's nothing wrong with this practice in itself, but when midsection training is left to the last moment, and you're rushed to finish your workout, or too tired to do justice to the area, you're not going to develop an impressive abdominal region. Answer: You have to pace your workouts, to allow adequate time, and save proportionate energy for a *complete* ab training section.

THE BEST ABDOMINAL EXERCISES

There are literally hundreds of waistline exercises, but like most professional body-builders I have my favorites. I use most of the following exercises, drawing on two or three every time I train my midsection. There are a few I don't use regularly, but which I've noticed work well for others. Every exercise works one part of a muscle more than another. For the sake of discussion, let's split up ab training into four different areas:

1. The upper abdominal wall
2. The middle abdominal wall
3. The lower abdominal wall
4. The intercostals

The upper abdominal wall is the easiest to develop. Next in order of easy-to-build is the midregion, with the lower abs below the navel being the hardest. Usually there is only one "ridge" of midsection below the navel, and only the best body-builders manage to get this area to show real development. The intercostals are worked fairly thoroughly with a variety of twisting movements. You can do specific twisting movements such as broomstick twists (standing or seated), or you can incorporate a twist into most regular midsection exercises.

The Crunch

This exercise works the central area of the abdominal wall. Make an attempt to touch the elbows to the knees during each repetition.

The Bench-Lying Leg Raise

Keep the knees slightly bent as you raise your legs up and down. Concentrate on *feeling* the exercise during the movement. The lower and middle abs are brought into play in this exercise.

Frog Kicks

A popular exercise for the entire midsection. Lean back to a forty-five-degree angle as you straighten the legs and you'll feel it in the lower abdominals.

Frog Kick (start)

Frog Kick (finish)

mer.

Hanging Leg Raise

You can perform this exercise (from a horizontal bar) with the legs straight or bent. The straight-leg version delivers higher intensity, while the bent-leg variation allows for a stronger concentration (squeeze) at the top of the movement.

Broomstick Twists

Place the broomstick bar across the back of the shoulders, keeping the hips facing the front, twisting the torso from side to side. This movement works the intercostals at the side of the waist.

Kneeling Rope Crunches

You need a lat machine for this one. Hold the rope or bar behind your head while kneeling; bend forward, crunching your abs as you do so. Rope crunches work the upper and middle midsection.

Bench Crunches (twisting)

Lying on your back on the floor, place your lower legs on an exercise bench, so that your upper legs are vertical. Partially sit up, twisting the torso as you raise and return to the lying position. This works the middle abdominal area.

Because the abs are not used directly in other body-part exercises, they can be trained at any time. You can still press, bench-press or curl yourself to exhaustion after vigorously exercising the abs. Still, some people train their abs on their off days because they are not tied in with other movements. Personally, I like to keep my rest days as rest days. The following are a few sample ab routines that you can experiment with:

MIDSECTION AB ROUTINES

	Sets	Reps
Routine 1		
Crunches (middle abs)	2	15
Seated frog kicks	3	20
Routine 2		
Lying leg raise (lower abs)	3	25
Bench crunches (middle abs)	3	15
Broomstick twists (intercostals)	2	50–100
Routine 3		
Hanging leg raise (lower abs)	3	12–15
Bench-lying leg raise (lower and middle abs)	3	20–25
Twisting crunches	3	20
Routine 4		
Kneeling rope crunches (middle abs)	2	15
Hanging leg raise (lower abs)	2	15
Bench crunches, twisting (obliques–mid abs)	2	15
Broomstick twists (intercostals, obliques)	2	50–100

If right now your abdominal muscles don't show up as finely delineated "bricks" of hard muscle, then take steps to change your routine. Work the abs vigorously, and remember that diet is the single most important aspect of getting those abs to show in the mirror— reduce those junk calories and the cut-up look you want will come sooner than you think.

MY PERSONAL ARMORY OF ABDOMINAL EXERCISES

Lying leg raise

Hanging leg raise

Crunches

Twisting crunches

Frog kicks

13

BUDDY
TRAINING

Methods and techniques have come a long way since the birth of progressive resistance training in ancient Greece, when Milo of Crotona picked up a young bull calf, hoisted it across his shoulders and walked around the Olympic area in Athens. Milo would perform this task daily, and as the bull grew in size and weight, so did Milo's muscles.

For hundreds of years, the primary purpose of resistance exercise was to prepare soldiers for battle. The warrior's level of fitness was a matter of life and death. In the nineteenth century strong men began to appear in Europe, and gradually the pastime gained popularity and became a popular vaudeville act, much like wrestling is today. Only in this century has resistance exercise been broken down into three distinct categories: Olympic weight lifting, power lifting and body-building. And only in the past few decades have all three of these disciplines gained popular acceptance. For many years coaches refused to allow their athletes to use any weight-training exercises or any method that built strength and muscle size. They feared it would adversely affect performance. But by the mid-1960s coaches began to change their point of view. Strength training was catching on with runners, swimmers, boxers, field athletes. . . . In fact, strength coaches were eventually hired to keep athletes strong for every sport imaginable. Today strength training is an important part of virtually every successful athlete's exercise routine, and now this interest has spread to men and women who may not want to add strength for athletic pursuit, but who recognize resistance exercise as a terrific tool for improving the quality of their lives.

Muscular fitness reduces your chance of being injured in other physical activities. It reduces nagging muscle aches and pains, improves posture, increases energy, strengthens internal organs and enhances the circulatory process. Proper training will enable you to feel better, perform better and look better.

There has been an explosion of interest in body-building in recent years, but with it problems have also come. Many people find it difficult to maintain a regular training routine. It's often difficult to find the time for complete workouts, and gym fees can be expensive. Even the idea of purchasing weights and benches for home use may be unrealistic. Either the money isn't available or else there simply isn't room in the house or apartment. Many people who have an interest in progressive resistance exercise can't afford to participate in it.

But all is not lost. Where there's a will, there's a way. There's an answer for anyone who can't afford a gym membership or who for some other reason is unable to train with modern equipment. It's *manual resistance* (MR), and it can be done just about anywhere. For most exercises, all you need is a training partner. Instead of conventional dumbbells and barbells, the partner offers the resistance. With a little bit of ingenuity, you'll come to understand how fantastic this method of training can be. MR can provide the same overload as machines, dumbbells or barbells. Resistance is resistance. Your muscles can't see if you're using a chin bar or a lat machine, a sandbag or a dumbbell. What's important is that you increase the overload every workout (if possible), and that when you can't increase the overload, you *try* to increase it. This means applying more resistance or repetitions, taking less rest between sets, or a combination of any of the three.

Sure, MR is not as workable as an organized weight program, but it's the next best thing.

If you *are* able to train in your own home setup or at a commercial gym, MR can still be used to supplement your regular training (especially when you're traveling and no equipment is available). You'll quickly discover that some MR exercises are superior to their equivalent using free weights. The two main advantages are:

1. *The muscles can be worked to total capacity for each rep.* We all know that in weight training the first few reps of any exercise are not done at full capacity. They are serving only to exhaust the muscular strength prior to positive failure. With MR, your partner (spotter) can tailor the resistance so that your first rep is at near-maximum effort, and the second, the third . . . and so on. Tension can be kept on the muscles at all times.

2. *Your partner can consciously vary the intensity within each rep,* *so that the resistance is adapted to the strength curve of the exercise being performed.* For example, when performing the side raise your partner would use considerable resistance at the beginning of the exercise, but as the arms arrived at the crucifix position, the resistance would have to be lessened slightly, then increased again as the arms were lowered.

There are disadvantages. Theoretically, MR is very sound, but people being people, problems can arise. Specifically:

1. Your partner should possess roughly the same strength and condition as yourself.
2. Some practice is needed to perfect the act of providing MR to your partner.
3. MR does not allow you to accurately calculate or record (beyond counting reps) the resistance offered (as is possible with disc-loading barbells and dumbbells and weight-loaded machines). You can, however, still use a journal to track exercises, reps, impressions of exercise intensity, muscular soreness, nutrition, etc.

GUIDELINES FOR PERFORMING M.R. EXERCISE

• Start with only one or two sets of MR until you are used to the method. Beginners should not use maximum intensity during the first few workouts.
• Take approximately three seconds to raise the resistance and four or five seconds to lower it.
• Perform twelve to twenty repetitions for each movement.
• Exercise each body part twice a week minimum, three times a week maximum.
• Maintain proper communication with your training partner, letting him know whether you need more or less resistance or (if you are the one offering resistance) how many reps you expect of him.
• Again, as I explained earlier, maximum benefit will be obtained if you briefly pause and hold at the point of contraction. The partner should apply more pressure on the downward movement so that the trainer fully benefits from the negative part of each exercise.

THE EXERCISES

Chest

Resistance push-up
Chest crunch
Lying flye

Back

Seated towel pull
Standing towel pull

Shoulders

Towel upright row
Side raise
Bent-over side raise
Two-arm press (leaning forward)

Biceps

One-arm curl
Towel curl

Resistance _Push-up_ (start)

Resistance _Push-up_ (finish)

Chest Crunch (start)

Chest Crunch (finish)

Lying Flye (start)

Lying Flye (finish)

Seated _Towel_ _Pull_ (start)

Seated _Towel_ _Pull_ (finish)

Standing _Towel_ _Pull_ (start)

Standing _Towel_ _Pull_ (finish)

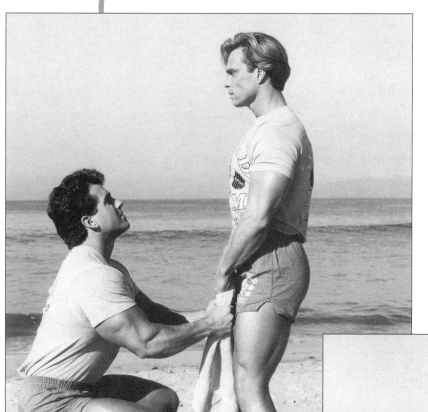

Towel Upright Row (start)

Towel Upright Row (finish)

Side Raise (start)

Side Raise (finish)

Bent-Over Side Raise (start)

Bent-Over Side Raise (finish)

Two-Arm Press (start)

Two-Arm Press (finish)

One-Arm _Curl_ (start)

One-Arm _Curl_ (finish)

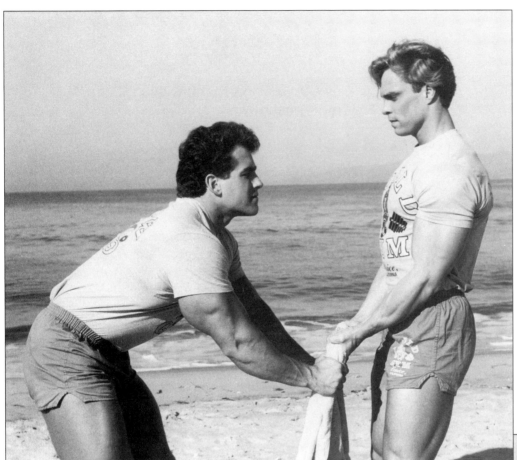

Towel Curl (start)

Towel Curl (finish)

Triceps

Towel extension (behind head)
Towel pushdown

Abs

Crunches
Lying leg raise

Hamstrings

Lying leg curl

Front Thigh

Sissy squat
Leg extension
Lunges

Calves

Standing calf raise
Donkey calf raise

Towel Extension (start)

Towel Extension (finish)

Towel Pushdown (start)

Towel Pushdown (finish)

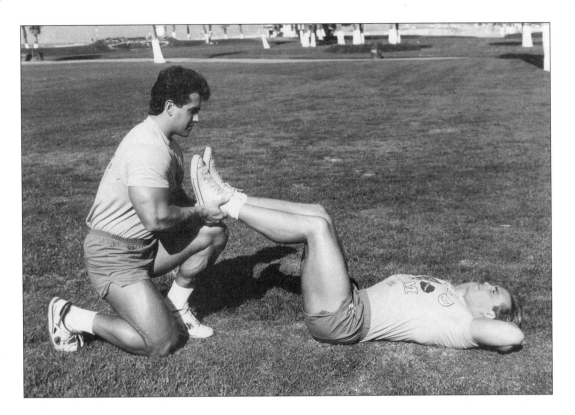

Crunches (start)

Crunches (finish)

__Lying Leg Raise__ (start)

__Lying Leg Raise__ (finish)

Lying Leg Curl (start)

Lying Leg Curl (finish)

Sissy Squat (start)

Sissy Squat (finish)

Leg Extension (start)

Leg Extension (finish)

Lunges (start)

Lunges (finish)

Standing Calf Raise (start)

Standing Calf Raise (finish)

Donkey Calf Raise (start)

Donkey Calf Raise (finish)

14

FAT-STRIPPING
AEROBICS

Let's suppose that you want to reduce your body fat, while maintaining muscle mass. How would you go about it? You would diet, right? Yes, reducing your calorie intake is important, but it's not the whole answer.

Until recently, body-builders lifted weight to increase muscle mass and dieted to lose body fat. There's a major flaw in this system that can prevent you from achieving your goals. About two weeks into a reduced-calorie diet your metabolism will begin to slow down. It's a survival mechanism that your body uses when it feels it's going to be starved. To continue losing weight you'll have to keep reducing your calories to match the metabolic slowdown. Because you'll be training with weights, the weight loss won't be as dramatic as for someone who diets without any type of exercise. I've seen body-builders who must go down under one thousand calories a day, though, because their metabolic rate has become so slow.

When the diet gets this severe you'll have very little energy for training and, consequently, you'll lose muscle mass. The way to lose body fat while maintaining or increasing muscle mass is to combine a sound diet with moderate aerobic exercise. Stationary bikes, stair-climbing machines, treadmills and aerobic rowers are becoming common equipment in almost every gym. My favorite moderate aerobic exercise is stationary biking. When I ride the bike I'm doing it only as a body-fat reduction exercise. I'm not trying to train my leg muscles. My goal is to raise my pulse rate to between 70 and 80 percent of its maximum, and to maintain it at that level the entire time I'm riding.

You can figure out your own ideal pulse range by first calculating your maximum heart rate. This is calculated by subtracting your age from the number 220 (220–your age = maximum heart rate). You would then multiply that number by .80 to calculate your own 80 percent range.

Many body-builders feel that any exercises done outside their regular weight workout will cost them hard-earned muscle size. This is only true if the aerobic exercise performed is too intense. If your pulse rate rises above 80 percent of your maximum heart rate, you will be using stored glycogen for energy. If you maintain your pulse in the 70–80 percent range, you'll be converting and burning your stored body fat as fuel.

If you do your aerobics as an all-out intense workout, you'll burn glycogen that would ordinarily fuel your weight workouts. You'll deplete your muscles and interfere with the muscle's recuperation times. Burning muscle glycogen outside your weight workouts will thus cause you to lose muscle size. Remember, all you're trying to accomplish by riding, walking or climbing in the 70–80 percent range is speeding up the metabolic rate.

I ride the bike between four and six days a week for twenty to thirty minutes at a time. I do this either immediately after my weight workout or at a separate time during the day. If I do my moderate aerobics at a different time from my weights, I can give myself an additional metabolic boost. The best thing about including moderate aerobic training in my routine is that I not only burn calories while riding, but my body continues to burn calories at an accelerated rate even after the workout is over.

When I do my stationary cycling, I don't try to see how much tension I can use or at how high a level I can ride. I use a low-to-moderate tension level and turn the pedals at between 90 and 100 revolutions per minute. If I get too much of a pump and burn in my front thighs, I know that I'm using too much tension. Your pulse rate should be the sole indicator of workout intensity. You don't need any fancy electronic

device to measure your pulse. Simply find your pulse by placing your index and middle fingers (first two fingers) on your neck, just to the side of your throat. Using an ordinary watch with a second hand or a digital second counter, count the number of beats while timing six seconds. In your head, add a zero on to the end of that number. If you counted fourteen beats in six seconds, you would add a zero on to the end and you would have a pulse rate of 140.

There is a secondary benefit of moderate aerobics for the body-builder. You'll improve your cardiovascular condition. You'll not only have lower body fat, but also a healthier heart and lungs. You will be fit on the inside and on the outside. I've observed that when my body is more fit, it also looks healthier. Combining weight training, a balanced diet and moderate aerobics will move you closer to the look you want.

15

OPTIMUM NUTRITION

Those of us living in the Western world are lucky enough to have a choice regarding the foods we eat. Accordingly, it's incumbent on us—especially those of us who want to reshape our bodies—to choose wisely. Common sense tells you that fresh foods, cooked with a minimum of processing, are best.

The kinds of foods to avoid on a regular basis are junk foods such as: french fries, butter, double cheeseburgers, fried chicken, chocolate Easter bunnies, soft drinks, powdered doughnuts—well, you get the picture. The more processed the food, the more you'll want to avoid it. Chances are very high that if you can get it at a drive-thru window it won't contribute to your long-term goals.

This isn't to say that you can't eat junk food now and again. Just don't fall into the habit of having it every day for lunch or midmorning snack. Irrespective of the long-term health hazards brought on by regularly eating junk food, these calorie-dense, fatty, often sugar- or salt-loaded items are not conducive to building healthy muscle tissue.

The question of when to eat, and how often to eat, can be confusing. It all depends on your caloric needs, your metabolism and your personal goals. If you're in doubt about when to eat, then eat only when you're hungry. And enjoy your food instinctively. Eat what your body craves, not what your mind craves. I myself have a structured way of eating, setting times aside to take my meals. But even though these guidelines are established in advance, I can't plan everything. When I'm especially careful to *make* time for eating (whether I'm catching a plane, traveling in a car or rushing between appointments) is when I'm preparing for a contest. At such times I'll always have my pre-prepared meal, and I'll eat it on time.

Though I try generally to follow a "clean" eating pattern, I do allow myself one day a week to have any food I want. Usually Sunday. When I first adopted this system years ago, I found myself dieting all week and then, on the given day, pigging out as if there were not going to be any food left next week, and putting on about ten pounds in that one day. Of course, I had to eat like a bird on Monday and Tuesday just to get back to where I was before Sunday's pig-out. I've since matured. Now my body craves clean food, so on my one day off I'll sit down to a *meal* off my diet—*anything* I want, but only for one meal and only until I'm just full, not exploding. This is the sanest way to be disciplined and yet flexible too.

Regarding junk food, there are three main ingredients you should be on the lookout for: salt, sugar and fats. Cut down on salt and table sugar. Fruits and vegetables contain plenty of natural sugars and salts (certainly enough to meet your needs). Honey is no better than sugar. Both are simple carbohydrates. Reduce your fat intake; avoid butter, cheese, mayonnaise and added oil. Most animal products and cereals contain more than enough fats. One of the curses of Western society is our habit of frying foods to make them taste better. Never forget: Fat makes us fat. Fried foods are not good nutrition for the athlete.

Let's take a peek at how the average North American eats: he skimps on breakfast because he hasn't organized his time to allow any time for breakfast preparation. At best he'll eat a processed cereal and chug down a coffee. Then on Saturdays and Sundays he'll stuff himself with smoked meat (bacon), fried eggs, fried potatoes, muffins, French toast, maple syrup . . . you name it. Lunch usually consists of a salt-loaded canned soup and a thickly buttered cheese or meat sandwich, washed down with a sugar-loaded soft drink. Dinner might be fast food (nearly always deep-fried) or perhaps a frozen dinner. . . . Almost all of the aforementioned foods are chosen for taste rather than nutritional value.

As a person who wants to make athletic gains, you must take the opposite approach. Don't look at food as something that merely fills the stomach and tastes good. Always ask yourself: Is it optimum nutrition? Will this food I'm eating contribute 100 percent to improving my mass, tone, shape and health?

In the past, body-builders were basically told to worship the god protein. The philosophy behind this was the athlete's credo: "Want muscle, eat muscle." We now know this isn't necessarily true. What happens is that the body utilizes the protein it needs for current tissue repair, but the calories that surround it are stored as fat. You need to find a balance in nutrition—a middle path that involves feeding the muscles completely but not excessively. Your key need is energy. You must have energy to train and recover. Glycogen in the muscle and liver is the key substance. The question is: How do you go about acquiring it? You need protein, yes, but ideally glycogen should come from a complex carbohydrate source such as whole grains and fresh vegetables.

An average weight-trained athlete should balance his or her food intake as follows: 65 percent complex carbohydrate, 20 percent protein, 15 percent fats. The competitive body-building athlete should take in 60 percent complex carbohydrate, 30 percent protein and 10 percent fats, throughout the year. As I suggested earlier, you may be able to afford a loose eat-what-you-like day once a week, but this practice doesn't suit everyone. Certainly you shouldn't go crazy and binge on that day. And it goes without saying that this isn't something you should do during a contest countdown, when you're systematically trying to lose *all* excess body fat. The following is a "clean food" sample diet:

✸

Meal One

Large bowl of oats or other hot cereal

2–3 ounces of nonfat milk

Raisin cooked in cereal

1 piece of fruit (banana, apple, peach)

1 whole egg, 3–4 egg whites (scrambled)

Coffee or tea (no sugar)

✸

Meal Two

*6–8 ounces of chicken breast or broiled round steak
(no higher than 7 percent fat)*

2 cups of rice (brown or white)

Cut-up vegetables (peas, corn, mushrooms)

Meal Three

2–3 pieces of fruit (bananas, oranges, apples)
½ cup of nonfat yogurt

Meal Four

6–8 ounces of lean beef, chicken or turkey
4 ounces of pasta (made without oil) with tomato sauce (not ketchup)
Small salad (lettuce, carrots, celery, tomatoes, cucumber)
Squeeze of lemon or limited amount of low-calorie dressing

Meal Five

2 pieces of whole-grain bread (no butter)
4–6 ounces of lean meat
Lettuce and tomato
1 apple

Protein/Carb Drinks

Use only if you need to replace a meal, or immediately after a workout if you know you are not going to be eating for over an hour. Drink it one-half hour after your training.

• Mix a high-quality milk and egg-protein powder with water to produce a shake. Add soft fruit such as bananas, strawberries, peaches, etc., to add carbohydrates and enzymes. It's very important to have both protein and carbohydrates in these drinks, especially if they're used as meal replacements. They can also be used by the athlete who wishes to eat five or six meals a day, yet doesn't have time to cook everything.

LOSING WEIGHT

Let's keep this simple: You don't have to count *every* calorie, but you should be aware of calorie values so that you know roughly how many calories you're ingesting.

To shed excess weight, calorie consumption should be reduced while keeping protein/carbs and fats in the same proportions. Eat clean food only. No calorie-dense foodless foods such as chocolate, butter, ice cream, cookies, candies, pretzels, potato chips or sweet desserts.

You must always be aware of the approximate breakdown of calories/fat/sodium/carbs. You don't have to be a fanatic and weigh all your food, calculating every last gram, but don't lie to yourself either. With time you'll learn instinctively how many calories are in that chicken breast, etc. . . .

The following is a table of popular foods showing their nutritional values. You can find more detailed charts listing hundreds of food items in the diet and health section of your local bookstore.

	Measure	Weight (g.)	Food Energy (cal.)	Protein (g.)	Fat (g.)	Carbohydrate (g.)
Milk, Cheese, Cream, Related Products						
Whole milk, 3.5 percent	1 cup	244	160	9	9	12
Nonfat (skim) milk	1 cup	245	90	9	tr.	13
Partially skimmed, 2 percent milk	1 cup	245	123	9	5	12
Ice cream: regular (approximately 10 percent fat)	1 cup	133	255	6	14	28
Yogurt (made from partially skimmed milk, plain)	6 oz	185	112	9	3	13
Yogurt (made from partially skimmed milk, fruit-flavored) (average)	6 oz.	185	170	8	3	30
Cheddar cheese (1-inch cube = 17 grams)	1 oz.	28	116	7	8	tr.
Cream cheese	1 oz. (2 tbsp.)	28	105	2	11	1
Whipped cream (pressurized, 18–26 percent fat)	1 tbsp.	3	10	tr.	1	tr.
Eggs, large, raw or cooked in shell:						
Whole egg	1 egg	50	80	6	6	tr.
White of egg	1 white	33	15	4	tr.	tr.
Yolk of egg	1 yolk	17	60	3	5	tr.
Meat, Poultry, Fish, Shellfish, Related Products						
Ground beef, broiled, lean	3 oz.	85	185	23	10	0
Round steak	3 oz.	85	220	24	13	0
Flank steak	3 oz.	85	245	23	16	0

	Measure	Weight (g.)	Food Energy (cal.)	Protein (g.)	Fat (g.)	Carbohydrate (g.)
Pork chop, lean only	1.7 oz.	48	130	15	7	0
Veal, cooked, bone removed: Veal cutlet or veal chop	3 oz.	85	185	23	9	–
Chicken, meat only (without skin) (1 cup diced = 5¹/₃ ounce)	3 oz.	85	115	20	30	0
Turkey, roast, meat only (without skin)	3 oz.	85	160	25	6	0
Beef heart (braised)	3 oz.	85	160	27	5	1
Fish: halibut, grilled	3 oz.	85	146	21	6	0
Fish: trout, poached	3¹/₂ oz.	100	167	18	10	0

Mature Dry Beans and Peas, Nuts, Related Products

	Measure	Weight (g.)	Food Energy (cal.)	Protein (g.)	Fat (g.)	Carbohydrate (g.)
Cashew nuts, roasted	1 cup	140	785	24	64	41
Peanut butter	1 tbsp.	16	95	4	8	3

Cereals and Cereal Products

	Measure	Weight (g.)	Food Energy (cal.)	Protein (g.)	Fat (g.)	Carbohydrate (g.)
Branflakes, with raisins and nutrients	²/₃ cup	28	100	2	tr.	22
Bread, cracked wheat	1 slice	3	77	3	1	15
Bread, dark, pumpernickel	1 slice	32	79	3	tr.	17
Bread, whole whea	1 slice	30	72	3	1	15
Cornflakes, plain	1 cup	21	80	2	tr	17
Macaroni, cooked	1 cup	140	155	5	1	32
Pasta	1 cup	140	155	5	1	32
Muffins, bran	1 muffin	35	86	3	3	14

	Measure	Weight (g.)	Food Energy (cal.)	Protein (g.)	Fat (g.)	Carbohydrate (g.)
Oatmeal or rolled oats, cooked in water	1 cup	240	130	5	2	23
Apple pie (crust made with enriched flour; 4-inch piece)	1 sector	160	410	3	18	61
Pizza (cheese; $\frac{1}{8}$ of 14-inch-diameter pie)	1 sector $5\frac{1}{2}$ inch	75	185	7	6	27
Pizza (sausage; $\frac{1}{8}$ of 14-inch-diameter pie)	1 sector $5\frac{1}{2}$ inch	105	315	14	17	27
Rice, white: unenriched, cooked, short grain	1 cup	170	215	4	tr.	50
Hamburger bun	1 bun	60	164	5	2	30

Fats and Oils

	Measure	Weight (g.)	Food Energy (cal.)	Protein (g.)	Fat (g.)	Carbohydrate (g.)
Butter	1 tbsp.	14	100	tr.	12	tr.

Vegetables and Vegetable Products

	Measure	Weight (g.)	Food Energy (cal.)	Protein (g.)	Fat (g.)	Carbohydrate (g.)
Asparagus, green pieces, $1\frac{1}{2}$–2-inch lengths	1 cup	145	30	3	tr.	5
Asparagus, cooked, drained	1 cup	125	30	2	tr.	7
Broccoli, cooked, drained: whole stalks, medium size	1 stalk	180	45	6	1	8
Brussels sprouts, cooked, 7–8 sprouts per cup	1 cup	155	55	7	1	10
Cabbage, cooked, finely shredded, small amount water	1 cup	170	35	2	tr	6
Raw cabbage, finely shredded	1 cup	90	20	1	tr.	5
Carrots, raw, $5\frac{1}{2}$ x 1 inch	1 carrot	50	20	1	tr.	5
Carrots, cooked, diced	1 cup	145	45	1	tr.	10

	Measure	Weight (g.)	Food Energy (cal.)	Protein (g.)	Fat (g.)	Carbohydrate (g.)
Celery, raw, 8 x 1½ inch large outer stalk.	1 stalk	40	5	tr.	tr	2
Corn, sweet, cooked, 5 x 1¾ inch	1 ear	140	70	3	1	16
Lettuce, raw, head 4¾-inch diameter	1 head	454	60	4	tr.	13
Peas, green, cooked	1 cup	160	115	9	1	19
Potatoes, medium, baked, peeled after baking	1 potato	99	90	3	tr.	21
Spinach, cooked	1 cup	180	40	5	1	6
Tomatoes, raw, 2 x 2½ inch or 7–8 miniatures	1 tomato	150	35	2	tr.	7
Cauliflower	1 cup	155	55	7	1	10
Red potato	1 potato	110	155	2	1	36
Vegetable juice, canned	1 cup	243	43	2	tr.	9

Fruit and Fruit Products

	Measure	Weight (g.)	Food Energy (cal.)	Protein (g.)	Fat (g.)	Carbohydrate (g.)
Apples, raw, 2½-inch diameter	1 apple	150	70	tr.	tr.	18
Apple juice, canned, vitamized	1 cup	248	120	tr.	tr.	30
Bananas raw, medium size, 7–8 inch long	1 banana	175	100	1	tr.	26
Blackberries, raw	1 cup	144	85	2	1	19
Blueberries, raw	1 cup	140	85	1	1	21
Grapefruit, raw, white, medium 3¾-inch diameter	1/2 fruit	241	45	1	tr.	12

	Measure	Weight (g.)	Food Energy (cal.)	Protein (g.)	Fat (g.)	Carbohydrate (g.)
Grapes raw, USA type (slip skin)	1 cup	153	65	1	1	15
Oranges, raw, 2 5/8-inch diameter	1 orange	180	65	1	tr.	16
Orange juice, fresh, all varieties	1 cup	248	110	2	1	26
Peaches, raw, whole, medium, 2-inch diameter	1 peach	114	35	1	tr.	10
Pineapple, raw, diced	1 cup	140	75	1	tr.	19
Raisins, seedless, packaged, 1/2 ounce or 1 1/2 tablespoon per package	1 pkg.	14	40	tr.	tr.	11
Raspberries, raw	1 cup	123	70	1	1	17
Strawberries, raw	1 cup	149	55	1	1	13
Watermelon, raw, 4 x 8 inch	1 wedge	92	115	2	1	27

Sugar and Sweets

	Measure	Weight (g.)	Food Energy (cal.)	Protein (g.)	Fat (g.)	Carbohydrate (g.)
Cake icings: chocolate made with milk and fat	1 cup	275	1035	9	38	185
Honey	1 tbsp.	21	65	tr.	0	17
White sugar, granulated	1 tbsp	11	40	0	0	11

Miscellaneous Items

	Measure	Weight (g.)	Food Energy (cal.)	Protein (g.)	Fat (g.)	Carbohydrate (g.)
Wines: table	3 1/2 fl. oz.	100	85	–	–	4
Cream of mushroom soup	1 cup	245	215	7	14	16
Tomato soup	1 cup	250	175	7	7	23

OVERLOADING THE STOMACH

If you eat too much, or make a habit of eating foods that don't agree with you, you run the risk of overloading your stomach. This can frequently happen if you ingest too many protein drinks or large amounts of milk. You can bloat your stomach and cause digestive irregularities.

Many people are allergic to milk products. Cow's milk is, after all, designed by nature to feed calves, not adult humans. But it can be a valuable food in limited amounts. If you've experienced allergic reactions in the past, you might try special milk products now being marketed that have additional enzymes intended to counter the problem.

Eating small meals (more frequently) is one answer to overloading the stomach. Don't eat a full meal straight after a heavy workout. The more intense the workout, the longer you're going to have to wait before eating (usually an hour to an hour and a half for a large meal). You should, however, snack within half an hour of training to replace depleted amino acids and glycogen.

RESTAURANT FOOD

Always choose a restaurant that has a wide variety of food on the menu—not McDonald's! Be polite but firm (you're paying for the food, after all) and simply ask the server for meat or fish broiled, no fat or salt; plain rice or baked potato (no butter, sour cream, sauces or gravies); or pasta made without salt or oil. Vegetables should be steamed or raw, but you also have the option of eating a salad with lemon and vinegar. Fresh fruit (not canned) makes for a tasty dessert.

If your server indicates he can't accommodate you (it happens), ask to see the manager and plead your case politely: "I have a terrible allergy to fat, salt and sugar. Can you please see what you can do for me? If I don't get food free of these ingredients, I'll drop dead." If the answer's still no, get up and leave.

People often ask me how they can eat during the day, given their job-imposed timetables. Truck drivers complain about having to eat at truck stops. Salespeople face similar problems. People from all walks of life and vocations feel it's not easy for them to eat properly. The answer, of course, is to prepare your meals at home in sandwich bags or plastic containers. Ideal foods to carry to work include fresh-cooked turkey or chicken breast (without the skin), white rice, rice cakes, vegetables or fruit. You can also put a protein/carbohydrate shake in a thermos, which will keep at a really cold temperature throughout the day.

I find that where food's concerned, it's very easy to slip into poor habits. When you're trying to eat clean, there are always plenty of family members and friends willing to sabotage your efforts. They do it under the guise of kindness. "How could you turn down those lovely cookies I've just baked for you?" "Just have one dish of dessert—it's very tasty. I'll be hurt if you don't try it!"

At such times you must remind yourself of the goals you've set. Remember: That off-diet day is never more than six days away. Keep the rewards of dieting clear in your head: good health, added fitness, clearer skin and a body that *gets noticed*.

Clearly, we all have foods we love but which we know we can't eat regularly. This is often the case with alcohol. I sometimes allow myself a glass of wine with my evening meal, or perhaps a light beer, but even this is not a regular thing. Every January to April I drink no alcohol at all. I like to clean out my system completely, sticking to water, tea or coffee, or limited amounts of diet sodas. I *don't* believe juices offer much value. Fruits should be eaten whole if possible (*exception*: protein/carbohydrate drink). It is actually better to eat the whole orange, rather than orange juice; the whole apple rather than the juice. Fruits contain pulp and fiber that are often lost when juice alone is ingested.

Be aware that so-called health foods are not always as healthy for you as you may think. For example, many bran muffins are loaded with oil or sugar—or both! Read labels carefully before parting with your hard-earned cash. If I had to pick a single food that's helpful to body-builders, I'd pick rice. It offers good nutrition, and it does a lot for the muscle-building process.

There's an old saying that "an apple a day keeps the doctor away," and as far as cholesterol levels are concerned the saying is right on the mark. Medical experts agree. Apples are rich in pectin, a jelly-like fiber that has proven to be superior to oat bran for very moderately lowering cholesterol levels in the body. Pectin also helps diabetics control their blood sugar, because it slows the rate at which sugar is absorbed through the stomach lining.

Since there is overwhelming evidence demonstrating a linkage between bad cholesterol and heart disease, it makes sense to incorporate generous amounts of pectin into the diet. One orange, a medium potato, a tomato, and a half a cup of soya beans add up to almost nine grams of pectin—enough, along with a low-fat diet, to bring about an 11 percent cholesterol drop in two weeks. Incidentally, pectin doesn't reduce the good HDL cholesterol (which helps the heart), nor does it adversely affect low-to-normal cholesterol levels.

HIGH-PECTIN FOODS

Food	Grams	Food	Grams
½ grapefruit	5.9	½ cup fresh strawberries	.75
Orange	3.36	Red cabbage	.63
½ cup soybeans	3.45	½ cup broccoli heads	.48
Carrot	1.73	½ cup peas	.34
Potato	1.65	½ cup raw spinach	.34
Pear	1.25	Plum	.30
Apple	.73	Peach	.30
½ cup brussels sprouts	.76	Tomato	.21
½ cup beans	.70		

Supplements and body-building—what's the answer?   One thing is certain: supplements come and go—today's rage is tomorrow's forgotten ingredient.   Remember the Vitamin E craze?   "E" did everything from helping the heart to curing skin blemishes.   It supposedly made us sexier and enabled us to use more oxygen and grow hair . . . and even cured stretch marks.   Very few of these claims held up.

Today body-builders are offered new supplements and new promises all the time. And—surprise!—not all the claims you read are 100 percent factual.

You should study the ads in the various muscle publications with care.   If the claims sound unbelievable, they probably are. . . . Let the buyer beware.

I don't believe in year-round supplementation.   I think the body responds better to supplements after a rest.   My philosophy is to keep general nutrition so high that supplementation offers at best only a slight edge.

If you make certain that your nutrition is always good, you can feel secure in the knowledge that you're healthy and will make the best possible gains.

I'm always being asked which supplement manufacturers are best. It seems to me that the bigger companies, the people who've been around a long time and survived the vigilance of the FDA (who are always on the lookout for supplement manufacturers who don't live up to their label statements or who make exaggerated claims), are more likely to produce a quality product than a newcomer.

If you wish to try the esoteric supplement, and if it's within your budget, then try it for a month. Keep all variables consistent, and if you *feel* and *see* results then the product *is* working for you. If there seem to be no results, then it's *not* working. There *are* good basic supplements out there. Balanced multiple amino acid formulas that have a similar amino acid profile to human muscle protein are a good bet. Amino acids are not drugs or chemicals; they're pure food. Even so, don't rush into taking large dosages. Practice caution when using aminos. Begin with just a few each day and increase the amounts slowly while you gather feedback data. You may not need large amounts to give your body the appearance you're looking for.

Free amino acid supplementation could be described as one of the essentials for the natural body-building enthusiast. These supplements have the unique feature of passing straight into the bloodstream without having to be digested. Correct ratios and balance are needed, though. The Colgan Institute of Nutritional Science has published papers in numerous leading scientific journals and has designed many nutritional programs for athletes and body-builders. The following are its findings of the amino percentages that are ideal for hardworking body-builders and athletes:

Essential Amino Acids (%)		Nonessential Amino Acids (%)	
Arginine	2.1	Alanine	3.6
Histidine	1.8	Asparagine	1.4
Isoleucine	9.1	Aspartic acid	5.5
Leucine	15.1	Cysteine	0.2
Lysine	5.4	Glutamic acid	13.4
Methionine	2.8	Glutamine	1.4
Phenylalanine	2.6	Glycine	2.9
Threonine	3.6	Ornithine	0.7
Tryptophan	0.7	Proline	8.7
Valine	12.7	Serine	5.7

Personally, I've experimented quite a bit with food supplements and have noticed measurable changes (e.g., more mass, greater definition, added separation), but I've *never* noticed miraculous results from taking supplements. Usually, when I take them, and everything else (training, rest, nutrition) is in line, supplements give me a slight edge. They're important, but they don't make a huge difference.

S U P P L E M E N T S

Useful

Vitamin C—For the support of the immune system and muscle recovery process.

B-complex—Key in breakdown, absorption and utilization of complex carbs. Complex carbs convert to muscle glycogen to fuel workouts.

Multimineral—Vitamins need minerals to be absorbed and utilized by the body.

Calcium-magnesium (in a two-to-one ratio)—Helps alleviate cramps.

Desiccated defatted liver—Increases muscular endurance.

Free-form balanced multiple amino acids—Taking a multi-amino is superior to using singular or even branch chain aminos, because you will be allowing your body to select what it needs from the full spectrum. The body tends to absorb amino acids in balance and will not utilize whatever it doesn't need.

Protein powder—Valuable as a source of amino acids. I sometimes use a protein/carbohydrate drink as a meal. A good protein powder should have aminos in correct ratio. Protein powders do *not* have magical qualities. They are a good supplement and should be used as such.

Possibly Useful

I've tried the following supplements and found them to have a limited amount of benefit:

Arginine-Lysine combination or *Ornithine*—Used as a growth hormone stimulator, taken at bedtime on an empty stomach.

Branch chain amino acids (Leucine, Isoleucine and Valine)—Taken immediately after the workout to replenish what was used during training.

Chromium—Helps to maintain a more even blood-sugar level while training. Chromium should be taken thirty minutes before a workout.

Spirulina—Contains the full range of amino acids. Possibly useful for people who don't eat meat.

Carbohydrates and electrolyte replacement drinks—Not particularly useful for body-builders. These supplements are better for endurance athletes performing for more than two hours' time, as glycogen and mineral replacements. Pure water is better for body-builders trying to replace fluids.

Weight-gain powders—Can be useful if you have a very fast metabolism and have a difficult time eating enough food to gain muscle. Since most are filled with pure simple sugars, this is my shakiest "possibly useful" supplement selection. I don't use weight-gain powders in my current supplementation.

Useless

I've tried all of these supplements under fairly constant conditions and found them to provide little or no results. Don't waste your money. This is only a partial list of supplements that are trendy as of publication: Smylax, glandular preparations (other than liver), dibencozide, ferulic acid, wheat germ oil, octacosanol, choline and inositol (as fat burners), inosine.

Above all, be guided by common sense. I've seen people get totally consumed by crazy nutrition habits. One California strong-man got so into carrot juice that he drank ten quarts a day . . . and turned orange. Another muscle-beach regular ate peanuts from dawn to dusk—he was even chewing during his bench presses. And then there was . . . well, I hope you get the message. Remember: *Balance* is one of my key words.

16

• • • • •

STEROIDS

• • • • •

When Rick Horgan of Warner Books asked me to write this book, one of the first decisions I made was to give as much detail about training and diet as I could, and hide nothing from the reader.

Unless you borrowed this book from the library or from a close friend, the likelihood is that you paid good money for it. To some, the cover price will be nothing, a mere pittance. To others, such as those who are attending school or college, the cost of *Beyond Built* will be substantial. Some of you will have gone without certain necessities to buy this. Others will have saved up to acquire it. This is all the more reason why I should honor your sacrifice, big or small, by imparting only the complete truth. Let's clear the air: Yes, I have used steroids, and done so under a doctor's supervision, and I didn't like it. It was part of the competitive environment I was in at the time.

I did put in years of hard work, before I even knew what anabolic drugs were. Steroids just weren't talked about in the media or the gym the way they are now. They're now painted as both magical wonder potions and deadly poisons. Generally, both of these arguments are made by people who have little idea what they're talking about.

Anabolic steroids have been playing some part in sports since the mid-1950s and perhaps even earlier. I'm sure, however, that if you were to ask an old-time body-builder if steroids were in use back then, he would claim otherwise. The route taken by many athletic champions has been to lie and even degrade all those who've indulged in this "evil." I believe that honesty is the only solution to what is becoming a complex problem. We need to shed light on the subject and separate fact from myth. When I realized that most competitive athletes were using anabolic steroids to enhance performance, I was confused. Everything I read about the sport pushed the idea of health benefits and sound body and mind. And yet here were athletes using "drugs." As time went on, I analyzed my potential as an athlete. I saw that I realistically had the chance to become a world-class competitor. I then acted as a rational adult and weighed the benefits of becoming a world-class champion against the possible harm I could do to my body. I looked at the sport and saw the competitive environment. I spoke at great length with several well-respected doctors specializing in sports medicine. Then I made a decision and took full responsibility for it. By this, I mean I looked not only at what effects steroid use would have in the short term, but also the ecology of their use over the long term. In other words, I looked at how they might affect my body by the time I was fifty or sixty years old. So under the supervision of the best sports-medicine M.D. I could find, I began limited steroid use. While using anabolics, I saw slight increases in strength and muscular size. However, there were no miracles. People often ask me if I experienced any side effects from steroid use. Fortunately, because of the limited doses and short durations of my times "on cycle," I never did feel any of the long list of potentially dangerous side effects.

At the same time, I began to see that maybe steroid use in sports was only there for the same reason I initially began using them: because of the competitive environment that existed. People took them because everyone else did. I wondered if there wasn't a possibility for change. One major reason change was necessary was the fan mail I was receiving from all over the world. Young athletes saw me as a role model. I wanted to help create an environment where they wouldn't have to decide whether or not to take steroids to become a champion. I was also becoming disillusioned with the implied necessity of anabolic use in order to remain a top professional body-builder. In 1985, I was the first male professional to write IFBB president Ben Weider, asking for drug testing in the men's professional events. The IFBB had used doping tests to monitor women's pro and amateur contests, as well as the men's amateur world championships. In 1990 the IFBB finally began testing the men's pro events, using state-of-the-art International Olympic Committee procedures. Yes, steroids are still out there, but they're more difficult to obtain, because many states forbid even medical doctors from prescribing them to otherwise healthy people. There are federal laws today that categorize anabolics with hard-core drugs such as cocaine and heroin, and in some instances gym pushers find themselves receiving jail sentences similar to those received by hard-drug pushers. I'm not writing this chapter to pass judgment on anyone, but I sincerely believe that it's hard work in the gym that builds a physique, not a couple of pills swallowed with breakfast.

If steroids didn't exist the same body-building champions we have today would still be champions. Because of their physical makeup, determination and consistent training, they'd still be on top. Champions have great heart and spirit. These are the ingredients for success, not anabolic steroids. That's being proven each year in the men's amateur contests and also in the Ms. Olympia, where competitive standards remain as high as ever. It's interesting to note that of the numerous countries that sell steroids over the counter without any type of prescription, not one of those countries has *ever* fielded a Mr. or Ms. Olympia competitor, let alone a winner. It's a documented fact that over one million athletes are currently using anabolics, both competitors and noncompetitors, so why don't we have a million Mr. Olympias walking the earth?

Steroid abuse is practiced mainly by body-builders who are noncompetitors. Their main goal in life is to be big and strong. Actually competing in a physique contest is not their primary goal, although some of these guys have the vague idea that they would like to compete one day and "blow everyone away. . . ." The truth is that they take so many steroids they couldn't compete successfully anyway. Heavy steroid dosages bunch up the shoulders, fatten the face, thicken the hips and greatly increase the waistline circumference. Steroid abusers *may* gain strength and size while on a heavy steroid cycle combining hundreds of milligrams of testosterone with half a dozen other anabolic drugs each week, but the moment they end the cycle they pee all those gains away and are right back where they began—except in worse health. Hardly the image of a trophy-winning athlete.

One of the scariest arguments against youngsters taking steroids is that the closure of the epiphysis is hastened, bringing about an end to linear bone growth. Teenagers taking steroids may halt their vertical growth.

Body-builders should be happy with the decision to dope-test both men's and women's physique contests. It's a step in the right direction that will change the image of the sport. Steroid testing is getting stronger and more efficient all the time. If you're hoping to compete one day then you'll inevitably be faced with drug testing. Don't kid yourself that you'll be able to beat the test when the time comes.

Current testing technology can detect some anabolic agents up to two years after use, and detection efficiency can only get better.

I feel that body-builders have taken a bad rap in connection with steroids because the results we get are more visible. We're not like sprinters or cyclists, who're judged on performance as opposed to appearance.

I'm definitely not in favor of anabolic use. I feel sorry for the youngster who barely a month into training is asking around for anabolic pills or shots. He's playing a serious game with his health, looking for miracles when only hard work and following the path from apprenticeship to mastery will get him the mass and shape he desires.

The following are some of the possible side effects associated with steroid abuse:

1. Loss of head hair in men and women (irreversible).
2. Increase of facial hair in women (irreversible).
3. Voice deepening in women (irreversible).
4. Clitoral enlargement in women (irreversible).
5. Increased likelihood of acne.
6. Enlargement of waistline.
7. Gynecomastia (feminizing of the nipple) in men.
8. Closure of epiphysis, halting linear bone growth.
9. Increased blood pressure (men and women).
10. Added likelihood of heart attack in later life.
11. Decrease in function of the immune system.
12. Increased possibility of liver damage.
13. Added likelihood of muscle and tendon tears, joint pains, stiffness, etc.
14. More chance of developing arthritis in later life.
15. Increase in frequency of anger and antisocial behavior, possibly leading to periodic uncontrolled rages.
16. Shrinkage of testicles.
17. Possible loss of sex drive.

I don't mean to alarm you with these possible side effects. There have been athletes such as myself who've taken anabolics in small doses and under a doctor's supervision who've suffered none of the above. On the other hand, there are many heavy steroid users who've known more of these side effects than they'd like to admit. There are no miracles! To succeed you must depend on three factors—steroids are not one of them:

1. Genetics
2. Work ethic
3. Spirit

17

PERSONAL CARE: THE MISSING INGREDIENT

My roots in body-building grew from a search. At seventeen I was searching for the perfect physique. I had a vivid picture in my mind of my body developed to its ultimate potential. With experience I learned that there was more to life than just workouts and that if I didn't develop other dimensions I'd end my life as a shallow, empty man.

Body-building was for me a metaphor, not only of physical development, but of full human development. If I had the ability to positively alter my physique, couldn't I also have similar effects on my mind and heart? I saw that the full development of my body, mind and heart created my spirituality. This full development was the one thing in life that I could truly own.

The balance that I sought led me to find things in nature, science, art and the human condition that might otherwise have gone unnoticed. The skills that I learned traveling the road from apprenticeship to mastery as a body-builder have served me in every area of life.

Skills such as passion, belief, work ethic, persistence, pride, competitiveness and flexibility—those same skills can be yours and can serve you far beyond the gym.

If there is one piece of advice that I can give to someone who asks, it is this:

Always strive to be a whole person. Just as you develop instinct to know what's right for you in the gym, develop your heart and learn to use it as your guide through life.

A major goal of this book, besides finding balance, is holistic care. "Take care of your body and it will take care of you."

It's not just enough to be *built*. The person who is *beyond built* knows how to care for him or herself in and out of the gym. Let's explore some other dimensions of achieving your own individual potential.

SKIN CARE

I grew up with the phrase "If you dance, you gotta pay the fiddler." Clichés aside, remember that there is a price for everything. If you spend your nights at a bar drinking shots of whisky and smoke three packs of unfiltered cigarettes a day, you're buying something. That something has a price tag. Most likely that price will be your life. But who knows, you might get a discount and only have to pay with a lung or a damaged liver.

It's surprising how many people feel that the possible loss of a vital organ isn't sufficient reason to learn self-love and to do away with destructive habits. But who am I to judge?

The skin on your body is also an organ. It is an organ that is going through constant change. Some people might argue that skin will just take care of itself. Oh, if only life were that simple.

These days, with what we're doing to our atmosphere, the rise in skin cancer is dramatic. All that pollution is eating away at the filter system (ozone) that keeps the sun from burning us up like overdone french fries.

We need the sun's rays for life itself. We've got to see, though, that there's a price tag for the suntan that you get to make yourself look and feel better. It's dangerous out there. Constant overexposure to ultraviolet rays (sunshine) can do to your skin what smoking will do to your lungs.

Sensible, protected exposure to sunshine will enhance your health, skin tone and radiance. But you *must* build up your exposure to the sun slowly and intelligently.

When I was in high school I went with a bunch of friends to Florida for spring break. The first day there I laid my winter-white body out in the sun for at least six hours. That night I couldn't move and I was so burnt that I had to waste three days of beautiful beach weather sitting in the shade—in pain.

Every time you burn your skin in the sun you increase your chances of getting skin cancer. The answer is to begin exposure slowly during a cool time of day (9:00–10:30 A.M. or 2:30–4:00 P.M.) and to use a sunscreen.

Sunscreens filter out most harmful rays, and are rated on a number system. For example, a #2 sunscreen allows you two times the unprotected exposure (#10 allows ten times, etc.). The fairer your skin, the more protection is necessary.

You can also get a "sun block" product that will protect tender areas like your nose, ears, etc.

If you're tanning for competition, here are a few tips:

1. Get as even a tan as possible: under the arms, on the sides, and even front and back. Turn and lie at all different angles in the sun.
2. Do not burn. It's better to take twice as long to tan than to fry and peel.
3. You must moisturize your skin after sun exposure. When you come in from the sun, shower. Pat your skin *partially* dry. While your skin is still moist apply a moisturizing lotion and allow it to air-dry.
4. Once a week give yourself a super-moisture bath. Draw a medium-hot bath. Add 1 1/2 cupfuls of baby oil. Soak in the tub for five to ten minutes. Don't use soap; towel-dry your skin. Also, don't dunk your head under water in this bath. You don't want oil on your face and in your hair.

The same rules of skin moisturizing apply even during times you aren't tanning. Moisturizing will offset dry winter skin as well.

FACIAL SKIN CARE

Skin care has become a billion dollar industry. There are so many products (creams, potions, lotions and goos) that it boggles the mind.

Being a firm believer in the basics and not wanting to spend a small fortune on skin products has led me to the following four-step process.

The first of the four steps involves exfoliation approximately every two weeks. You'll want to use a facial scrub to remove the dead cells and help unclog pores. You should use a basic "grainy"--type scrub that is available from a skin-care professional, major department store or health food store. All skin-care products should be hypo-allergenic, and contain no perfumes or unnecessary additives. If you're being charged a lot of money for some "secret, magic" ingredient, be suspicious. There's a 99 percent chance you're being ripped off. Stick to the basics. Follow the directions on the container or consult a skin-care professional. The scrub, of course, is used every two weeks or so, but you must develop a day-to-day habit consisting of three steps performed morning and night. The entire process takes about three or four minutes.

The second of the four steps (first step in the daily plan) is cleansing. Using a hypo-allergenic face soap or cleanser and mildly warm clear water, wash your entire face and neck. Make sure to especially cleanse areas where pores might easily be clogged, such as on and around the nose and the forehead. Be sure to rinse thoroughly with clear water. Always cleanse your face before shaving, because the warm soap and water will soften your whiskers for a much smoother shave. Your beard will thank you.

The third step (second *daily* step) is toning. Toning is used to mildly remove dead skin on a day-to-day basis as well as to close and tighten pores. Toning will depend on your skin type. Does your skin flake and peel on the nose and forehead? It's probably dry; you'll need a very mild toner. Look for one that's either alcohol-free or very, very low in alcohol, so you don't dry your skin further. If your skin is oily you can use the same type of toner mentioned above, but you can also get away with one that's slightly more astringent (containing more alcohol) to further tighten pores and remove excess oil from the skin. Please be aware, though, that some skin oil is normal and necessary for proper skin health and elasticity. So don't turn your face into sandpaper trying to do away with all that "nasty" oil. You'll cause more problems than you solve.

The fourth and final step (third *daily* step) is moisturizing. The purpose of moisturizing is to hold water against the skin so that the skin is fully hydrated. Facial moisturizer should be very light. You don't need to spend your savings to get a good product. On the other hand, don't just pick up the generic hand cream at the supermarket and smear it all over your face. The key areas for moisturizing are

1. At the "smile lines" corner outside the eye.
2. For men who shave, on the beard area.
3. Very lightly on the forehead, neck and cheek areas.

A R E A S   T O   A V O I D

1. The soft tissue directly under your eyes.
2. If you have easily clogged pores, on and around the nose, on the forehead or on the chin.

The method you use to moisturize is extremely important and often overlooked. Remember, you're trying to trap water against the skin to keep it moist. If you just put moisturizer on dry skin, this will not be accomplished. After toning, allow toner to mostly dry, then moisten your face with clean water. While your skin is still moist, apply a very small amount of moisturizer to the needed areas and allow your face to air-dry.

Attention, macho men: Real men *do* use the four-step process. Especially if they don't want to look seventy-five when they're thirty.

HAIR CARE

The days of the dollar haircut are gone. When I was a boy I was taken to the barbershop, put up on a booster seat in the barber's chair, and given a "number 3" on the wall chart of haircuts. Of course, numbers 1 through 5 were all variations of the crewcut. Number 3 happened to be called "the Buzz Job." Electric clippers were the tool of the day, and butch wax held my quarter-inch bristles in place. Long hair (longer than three-fourths of an inch) was for women, hippies and sissies. Of course, my father was bald, which could account for his uncontrolled need to make me so, too. He gave the barber a dollar while I hopped down from the chair.

Judas at least got several silver coins for his dirty deed. In case you can't tell, I don't hold fond memories of my boyhood barbershops. It's especially confusing when I now see young teens asking to voluntarily get "the Buzz Job" that I so hated as a boy. But styles change.

My main concern now is finding a hairstylist who does a quality haircut that complements the shape of my head and texture of my hair. It was a hairstylist who convinced me that I was ruining my hair by using "supermarket shampoo." He made me realize that when a shampoo sits on a shelf for a long time, it must be loaded with additives and preservatives to maintain shelf life. Not only are these bad for the scalp, but ultimately, of course, they end up in the rivers and ocean. At first I thought I was being misled when he suggested using a reputable shampoo and conditioner that was sold either in a salon or beauty-supply store. But I decided that healthy hair was worth a little bit of extra money.

When you decide to get your hair cut or styled, it really pays to seek out the best and most reputable salon in your area. It doesn't have to be the most expensive. When you see someone with a hairstyle you like, ask him or her who does it. You'll be complimenting that person *and* gaining useful information.

When you arrive at your appointment, *talk* before you allow the stylist to cut. Discuss at length how you want your hair to look. How long do you want it? Do you want it long on top and short on the sides and back? Or do you want it all one length so you can grow it out?

Come to an agreement on the style before the scissors touch your hair. Also, consider this: You can always have more cut off, but you can't glue back on what's been cut too short. So feel free to interrupt if the stylist seems to be getting a bit boisterous. When he's finished cutting, blow-dry your hair the way you plan to wear it day to day and decide if you like what you see. How does it match your head shape and the image you want to project? If it's not right, politely but firmly ask the stylist to make changes until you're finished. When your standards have been met, tip the stylist 15 to 20 percent of the haircut fee.

The best hairstyles for athletic, active people are low-maintenance styles—in other words, something you can shampoo and quickly blow-dry after a workout, without a lot of fussing. It's important when active to shampoo your hair daily. When you work out, oils and gunk build up on the scalp, which can block the hair follicles and kill the hair roots. When you're showering or bathing, lather once with a good-quality shampoo and rinse thoroughly with lukewarm water. It's important when you shampoo to do a little exercising of your scalp. Don't just rub the shampoo around with the palms of your hands. Use your fingertips and massage your scalp. Move the skin back and forth and stimulate the blood flow all over your head as you lather. Maintaining a "loose" scalp with good blood circulation (which will result from massage) will improve the health and longevity of your hair. Most shampoo bottles say to lather and rinse twice but this is usually unnecessary unless your hair is extremely dirty. Remember, shampoo companies want you to buy their product. If you lather twice, you'll run out and have to buy more in half the time.

Depending on your hair type, you'll want to consider using a conditioner one or two times per week. The drier or more damaged your hair, the more frequently you'll need to condition it. This will also depend on the humidity in your area, as well as the level of air pollution. Conditioning can help hair damaged by dry, smoggy air. You should condition *after* shampooing and rinsing thoroughly. Use a conditioner specifically designed for hair (as opposed to a body moisturizer) and work it through your hair and into your scalp with your fingertips. Leave the conditioner in your hair two to five minutes and then rinse it thoroughly with lukewarm water.

A certain amount of dandruff is normal, but heavy dandruff is not. If you have chronic heavy dandruff, use a commercial dandruff shampoo daily, followed by conditioning as described above. If your dandruff persists, see your family doctor or a dermatologist. There are prescription treatments for bad scalp problems.

You may also want to supplement your diet with some extra vitamin C, E, selenium, B complex and zinc to improve hair health.

Another aid to healthy hair is getting outdoors. The sun, wind and natural elements will help the health of your hair.

Just make sure that when you arrive home from the beach or pool you wash your hair to get rid of salt or chlorine residues. Remember also that overexposure to the sun can fry your hair just like your skin. Rub a dime-size dab of conditioner around in your hands and run it through your hair for protection if you're planning extended sun exposure. This can act as a sunscreen for your hair. Of course, you should shampoo and rinse thoroughly as soon as you're back inside.

It's also a good idea to cover your head with a loose-fitting cap or hat when you're out in the hot sun. A head covering should be very well ventilated so that air can circulate. A tight hat worn all the time will act to "kill" your hair by not allowing your scalp to breathe. So hats should be used for limited purposes and short durations.

Once you've washed your hair, towel dry it, not with vigorous and violent rubbing, but by using the towel to soak the water from your hair. Putting the towel over your head, gently grab handfuls of hair through the towel and squeeze, allowing the towel to soak up the water. Once this is done, style your hair into place using a wide-toothed comb. If you use a brush on wet hair, you'll run the risk of hair breaking. At this point it's up to you if you want to style any further or just let your hair air-dry. Letting your hair air-dry is the healthiest thing to do, but in today's fast-paced world, most of us don't have time to sit around waiting for this process to take place. So we blow-dry. Blow-drying is here to stay—that is, until some technology replaces it, like microwaves for the head.

Blow-drying your hair gives you a lot of options. In cold weather you don't have to go outside with wet hair. You can be ready to rush out the door for a business meeting, school or a date. You also can have more flexibility as to how you style your hair.

The downside of using a blow dryer is that you can damage your hair. My recommendations are as follows:

1. Use a cool-to-medium temperature setting. Long-term hot-drying will fry your hair.
2. Allow yourself at least two times per week where you just let your hair dry naturally, without blow-drying.
3. When you blow-dry, your need for moisturizing conditioners increases. Be sure to condition at least once a week.

Thinning Hair

Male-pattern baldness (MPB or alopecia) is an inherited trait for which there is no cure. Scientists are searching, but so far they haven't found any cures for this condition that affects many men and some women. Male-pattern baldness can begin in some men as early as sixteen years old. There are, of course, many other reasons for hair thinning and loss.

The main, and most obvious, reason for hair loss is the death of the hair root. This can be caused by:

1. *Heredity*: male-pattern baldness.
2. *Trauma*: severe illness or drug reaction.
3. *Clogged pores at the follicle*: buildup of sebum and gunk on the scalp, combined with tight scalp skin.

If your hair is thinning for this third reason, chances are good that you can act to save and completely or partially restore your hair. Use this ten-step process to rebuild strength in your thinning hair.

1. Wash your hair daily using a high-quality salon shampoo.
2. Use your fingertips to vigorously massage your scalp while you're shampooing.
3. While shampooing, move your scalp skin back and forth and all around, relaxing your head. Studies show that a "loose" scalp is necessary for hair health and maintenance.
4. Rinse your hair thoroughly, using clean, clear, lukewarm water, after shampooing and conditioning. Use your fingers to move clear water down to your scalp to ensure there is no remaining residue.
5. Before washing your hair spend a couple of minutes brushing your hair in different directions. Brush your scalp also, but gently!
6. Do not wear tight-fitting caps or hats. Let the sun, wind and air get to your hair.
7. From time to time use your fingers to massage your scalp. Massage puts blood at the hair root, helping to stimulate growth.
8. Never pull a hair out by the root (even if it's gray). It won't grow back.
9. You can, however, use gentle pulling pressure to strengthen the hair root. Go around your head, section by section, and gently pull against a tuft of hair. This gentle pulling will help strengthen the root, in the same manner that curling a weight will strengthen a bicep.
10. If you use gel or spray for styling, keep it to an absolute minimum and always wash your hair thoroughly afterward to avoid buildup on the scalp.

If you have hair loss because of M.P.B. or trauma, all of the rules of healthy hair care still apply.

I happen to think there's nothing at all wrong or degrading about thin hair or baldness. For many it's simply a natural life occurrence. It is up to you to decide what your best course of action is if your hair loss is permanent.

Obviously, the best action would be total acceptance and integration. This involves learning acceptance of the person you really are, integrating into your high self-esteem those things that you can't change on an organic level. In other words, if there's no way on earth you'll grow new hair, you must either positively integrate this or find a way outside your own natural regenerative (organic) means to replace it.

There *are* means available. Natural-looking hair replacement procedures are becoming an art form. I know of one fellow professional who felt he was too young to integrate his hair loss. He researched and found a state-of-the-art hair replacement system. The hairpiece he was fitted with looks natural and is very functional for him as an athlete. He's so pleased with the results that it's added greatly to his self-esteem.

Hair replacement is definitely one place where you'll want to seek professional consultation and a company of impeccable reputation. On the other hand, if you decide to integrate your hair loss, look for a hairstylist who can advise you on the best cut for your head shape and facial features. You can still have your hair styled to make the absolute most of your looks.

Remember also that there are a number of celebrities who are considered handsome and sexy while sporting a bald head.

So if your hair is thinning, follow those ten steps to healthier hair. If you have already lost your hair, work to find the method that will boost your self-esteem, whether it's integrating your hair loss or finding a good hair replacement system.

Words of Caution: Any time there's a human condition that causes people anguish, there'll be those "entrepreneurs" (read "sharks") out there willing to feed off the hopeful. At this time there are no sure cures for permanent hair loss. If a real one came along, you'd probably learn about it on the front page of your local newspaper. Don't get ripped off!

THE TOTAL LOOK

Call me a blue-jeans, cowboy-boots and T-shirt kinda guy. If you see me walking around, 90 percent of the time this is how I'll be dressed.

That doesn't mean I don't like to "dress up." I do...sometimes. In fact, in the body-building world, I've somehow managed to develop a reputation as being well dressed. Interestingly, if you take a good look at someone considered to be well dressed, you may notice that it's not how expensive or trendy his clothes are that creates the illusion. That is, after all, what being well dressed is: an illusion. This illusion becomes particularly important as you develop your physical potential. Being built

is one thing, but let's go a few steps further. The most important thing when you've built your physique and want to clothe it is the fit.

Don't use the excuse that you don't want to build your body because you won't be able to find clothes that fit. It's an excuse and only an excuse. Put it in a different light: With a well-built body the clothes you wear will look that much better. You just have to put a little bit of effort into finding what's right for you. As you perfect your physique, you'll develop proportions that are a "tailor's nightmare." If you have legs that are only a few inches smaller than your waist, you can't just slip into any old pair of jeans on the shelf. You'll need to be selective. Fortunately, many casual-wear companies are making adjustments in their sizing and proportions to account for athletic builds. When you buy jeans, try them on. Don't just go by the waist size. You've got to make sure that they comfortably fit your thighs or else you're just wasting your money. Also, take into account whether the denim has been pre-shrunk. I've found two brands of "normal" blue jeans that fit me very well. I found them by patiently shopping and trying on pair after pair. When you're in a clothing store, don't be shy—ask the salesperson for help. Explain your dilemma. You might be

surprised to find that you're not the first person to ask the question. If the salesperson is not helpful or receptive, ask to speak to the store manager.

I tend to get a bit impatient when shopping for clothes. I'll give a store a chance, and if it doesn't suit my needs I'll find another. Oversized clothing is not just a fashion trend anymore. Companies are now making oversized shirts and large leg pants on a regular basis. You can also look through *Muscle and Fitness*, *Flex* or *Ironman* and find mail-order companies that cater to body-builders.

My experience with "Big and Tall" stores has not been good. Generally, the clothing is fifteen years behind current fashion. Also, you should know that these stores make clothing for big and tall people and not necessarily for athletic

physiques. They can carry useful items, such as two- or three-times-extra-large T-shirts or work shirts. Many of these stores are beginning to change as the market changes, so don't give up hope yet.

I usually shop at trendier-type chain stores that seem to stock oversized, basic, good-quality clothes. Two of the stores that immediately come to mind and are national are The Gap and Banana Republic. Both carry good selections and usually have some oversized things. Banana Republic has shorts that have big legs and recently carried great oversized, 100 percent cotton, solid-color T-shirts. The Gap sells my current favorite blue jeans. I can't get my legs into regular 501 buttondowns. The Gap jeans have bigger legs and fit in the waist. The company Marithé & Francois Girbaud also makes a variety of jean and pant styles that have big legs combined with normal waist sizes. All three of these companies offer high-quality goods at reasonable prices.

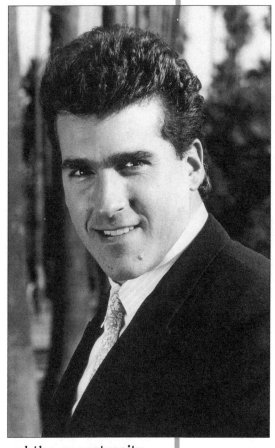

When I'm looking at buttoned dress shirts, the first thing I check is the arm size. I like there to be some bagginess in the upper arm. I think it's tacky to see a body-builder stuffed into a dress shirt with the arms and shoulders exploding. I've found that it's easiest to have dress shirts custom-made to ensure a good fit. It's not that much more expensive and is often cheaper than a quality off-the-rack shirt. If I'm happier with a great piece of clothing, I'll gladly pay a bit more for it.

If you have trouble buying suits, you might want to consider finding a reputable tailor and spending some extra money. I have to have my suits custom-made, because the last time I took a jacket off the rack, it started off resembling a tent that would comfortably accommodate a family of five and their dog. I then tried to have it "taken in," and the monstrosity went from bad to worse. I wound up using it to cover my car at night.

The type of clothes you buy will obviously depend on your needs. Examine your priorities. What do you wear to work? How are you comfortable during leisure time? Do you need expensive suits in your wardrobe, or will a sportcoat do? Or can you do just as well with a jean jacket?

Requirements of jobs and social life aside, you must dress to please one person—you. Of course, you want to look good for your spouse or your girlfriend or boyfriend, but when it comes right down to it, if you feel like a "million bucks," that's exactly how you'll come across. (Even if that "million bucks" is wrapped up in a pair of jeans, flip-flops, and a baggy T-shirt.) What's ultimately important is your own self-image. I'm not a big believer in chasing every fashion trend that comes along. The bulk of my "dressy" and "casual" wardrobe is made up of basic and timeless clothing items.

What I will do is buy one or two trendy things that really catch my eye each year and integrate them into my wardrobe. I also have a habit

that dates back to the days when I was on a very tight budget: I try to overlap as much of my clothing as possible. Apart from my jeans and T-shirts, I'll buy my clothes so that they are as interchangeable as possible. I'll try to find common hues of color in shirts, ties and pants so that I can create several outfits out of a few pieces of clothing. This doesn't have to be as boring as it sounds. Just use your imagination to mix and match colors and fabric textures. When I go into a store to buy a shirt I'll keep in mind what I already have in my closet, and buy accordingly.

When I first moved to California I was dirt poor. I had to make sure that every piece of clothing I owned would last. I think I was the only eighteen-year-old kid around who was meticulously following the care instructions on the inside garment tag. I mean, sometimes I didn't know where my next meal was coming from, much less my next shirt.

Those tags inside your shirts and pants are there for a very good reason. I learned this lesson the hard way, when I popped a brand-new all-cotton shirt (which I'd saved months to buy) into a hot washer and dryer. This wonderful, freshly laundered XXL shirt that I'd done without liver tablets in order to buy wound up fitting your average seven-year-old. Read the labels carefully.

18

PRECONTEST TRAINING

In the weeks following a contest I'm usually scheduled for guest-posing exhibitions, so I stay in tight shape until I've fulfilled these obligations. After the last commitment I take a break from pushing excessively in my workouts. I may even take time off for hiking in the mountains around Olympia, Washington, which is where I now make my home. I still eat healthy foods, but calorie counting is not a priority. Generally, I just do what I want. There are no pressures, no deadlines. Any exercise I perform will be done simply for the sheer joy of involving my body in strenuous physical exertion. This is *phase one* of my training year. It lasts two to three months, depending on how soon I get the urge to train with total commitment—to aim for a specific goal. The important thing is that I never force myself back into hard training. I let the motivation return naturally. Enthusiasm for hard workouts always knocks at my door sooner rather than later.

Phase two of my annual training is termed the *Growth Cycle*. This period lasts about six months and is the basic training that forms the foundation of the physique that's presented on stage at the culmination of the final cycle (phase three). During phase two I make a point of eating clean food (no fried food, very few junk items). I try to increase body weight, but with an eye on the amount of body fat gained. I can't emphasize enough the importance of keeping your body-fat percentage relatively low. If you allow yourself to gain excess weight, it makes achieving an ultra-ripped physique all the more difficult when you try to peak for a contest. There are many potentially good body-builders out there who can't get in shape for an event because they start their diets too late and never achieve their proper condition by contest deadline.

It's during phase two that you should concentrate on weak body parts. If phase two isn't performed with dedication; if you don't put in regular, quality workouts—increasing intensity, and addressing the problems of proportion and balance—then your final cycle, the *Peaking Phase,* will not deliver the physique you want.

Phase three is deadly serious, and it's typically begun twelve to fifteen weeks prior to competition. This is the time to be somewhat selfish, to turn your thoughts inward. No one can afford to treat the peaking phase lightly. You have to devote body, mind and soul to the task at hand.

As you enter the Peaking Phase you should be at your strongest and healthiest, with maximum size and corrected proportions. If you've done your job, your body-fat percentage will be relatively low. Certainly it shouldn't have been allowed to rise excessively. You have to change your diet at the outset of this phase, but slightly at first. You don't want dramatic losses in body weight, nor do you want to throw your metabolism into shock. Too drastic a cut in calories can fool the body into thinking a period of starvation awaits. This results in the body taking evasive action, all of which may translate into the slowing down of the basal metabolic rate (BMR). This has the effect of inducing your system to hold on to fat stores rather than shedding them. The diet should always be changed slowly. This is vital whether you're changing the content or the quantity of your diet.

As you get into the Peaking Phase you'll probably need to lose more body fat. Training intensity should be increased, because your objective is to hold on to previously built muscle mass while losing body fat. It should not, however, be increased to the point of overtraining. Remember to learn to read your body's signals. The majority of competitive body-builders will concede that some muscle mass is unavoidably lost during the pre-contest phase of training. You can minimize this muscle shrinkage by not letting yourself get too fat in the first place; by keeping your training intensity high; by balancing your protein, fat and carbohydrate intakes according to your needs; by making sure recuperation is at peak efficiency; and by reducing calories at a very slow rate.

This is the time when you need to start working on the posing routine and the tanning process. You must practice visualization, meditation and relaxation, the latter to help recovery during a phase when you're particularly vulnerable to exhaustion. There's no substitute for adequate preparation. By doing your homework, you'll increase your confidence, and your best performance will come when you're able to relax completely just before going on stage.

Typically, an athlete needs to be in shape two to four weeks prior to competition date. He can then make minor adjustments, add or lose weight according to his needs, by balancing his diet. The days of bulking up to thirty pounds or more above contest weight and then "cutting up" are over. This method never yielded the kind of finished look that is prevalent today.

It's impossible to bulk up and diet off the fat in six to eight weeks. At my best I was in shape two weeks before my show, and I just kept getting harder and harder. I saw Holland's Berry DeMey cut up in a similar way before entering the Olympia in 1988. He was in shape a good ten weeks before the event, and each day saw him harden even more. One of the secrets of coming to a show in shape is following a clean nutrition plan throughout most of the previous year. As the contest draws closer you should follow a diet of 60 percent complex carbohydrate, 30 percent protein and 10 percent fat. Calorie intake will fluctuate, because you'll be juggling the amounts of food you eat according to what the mirror tells you. Don't become addicted, though, to weighing yourself or taking measurements; neither mean a thing. Occasionally you may want to measure your body-fat percentage (with calipers) just to confirm that you're heading in the right direction. If you're using this as a measurement of progress, though, be sure to measure the exact areas each time in order to keep consistent data.

I'm often asked if I believe in the practice of carbohydrate depleting, followed by a period of carbing up. Well, I tried it and it didn't work. I wouldn't recommend it. You *could* try taking in a slightly higher percentage of complex carbohydrates, i.e., 75 percent carbohydrates, 20 percent protein and 5 percent fat, for a day or two, but today's top bodybuilders seem to be moving away from a strategy of totally depleting all carbohydrates for two or three days prior to loading.

As a competitive athlete I have to constantly redesign my diet and exercise plans. Always, the most important criterion is to make these routines serve my specific needs, and not to allow conventional practices to interfere. For example, I won't allow man's design of the seven-day week to hinder or handicap my training frequency, nor will I permit the breakfast, lunch and dinner custom to force me into the three-big-meals-a-day syndrome. This is very important if you want to be the best you can. And that's what this book is all about: achieving your fullest potential.

Here's my pre-contest diet: note that I haven't fallen into the breakfast, lunch and dinner habit.

✸

Meal One

Large bowl oatmeal with water

$1/2$ banana

1 whole egg, 6 egg whites (no salt, scrambled in Pam
or nonstick pan)

1 coffee, strictly no sugar or cream—sweetener is permitted

✸

Meal Two

Chicken or turkey breast (or occasional lean beef)

2–3 cups rice (I use brown rice if not before a contest, otherwise
white rice, which has less fiber and therefore doesn't give
such a full feeling)

1 cup coffee, no cream or sugar

✸

Meal Three

6 ounces lean meat (chicken or turkey)

1 large baked potato

Small salad (lemon and vinegar only, no dressing)

✵

Meal Four

4–6 ounces fish (orange roughy, cod or halibut)

Mixed vegetables (red potatoes, cauliflower, broccoli, zucchini)

No salt, but seasoning may be added: garlic, onion, etc.

In between meals I like to drink plenty of fresh water. This keeps the system flushed out and helps keep the body's internal mechanisms in top working order. After all, over 70 percent of your body is composed of water. Make a habit of drinking eight to ten glasses of water a day. Half an hour before each meal I also take a balanced complex amino acid formula (four or five capsules, four times daily). I also take the same amount (four or five capsules) immediately following a workout.

I believe in taking other vitamins, a few at a time, with my meals, but I don't advise, nor do I take myself, large dosages. In addition to a calcium/magnesium supplement that I take in a two-to-one ratio (emphasis on the calcium) to prevent leg or abdominal cramps, I also take vitamin C (for the immune system), B complex, and multiminerals. Without minerals the body won't absorb the vitamins.

As I said before, pre-contest training should be slightly more intense, but what will make it particularly rigorous is the lack of rest days. I try to compensate for lost rest days by maximizing the quality of my nontraining hours. Toward that end, there's a valuable technique I touched on earlier in this book that involves "breathing yourself down" to a super-relaxed state. You should start by sitting upright in a comfortable chair, or lying on the floor. The next step is to breathe in slowly through the nose (to warm and filter the air), feeling the air pass from the belly to the rib cage. You should endeavor to find your tension spots, and really relax. Using your mind's eye, imagine you're scanning yourself from head to toe with a laser beam scanner. Slowly now. . .as you "feel" a tension spot, make a conscious effort to think the tension away by super-relaxing the area, all the time breathing deeply and methodically. The more you can relax, the faster you'll gain complete control of your tension spots. Once you achieve a super-relaxed state, run a movie loop through your uncluttered mind, visualizing yourself posing successfully in front of a crowd. This is a sure way to replenish depleted energy and motivation.

During the last two weeks before a contest I keep my sodium (salt) level absolutely as low as possible. My relatively high water intake, however, is maintained right up to the night before the contest. If I cut down on water drinking too many days before the show, there's a tendency for the body to go into its survival mode, and store the water under the skin, so I keep my intake high until the day of the show. Remember, muscle is 70 percent water. Fat cells contain only 15 percent water, so if you chase out the water content of your body you lose more muscle than anything else.

If you travel to your contest by plane, make sure you take your own food (skinless chicken, rice, a few pieces of raw vegetables). When flight attendants see me eating my own stuff, they're confused. "Are you on some kind of diet? Can we help? Would you like some . . . " The answer has to be no. Even though you can order special meals on airlines (such as low-fat, low-sodium, etc.) if you call one day in advance, it's better not to risk what the airline's idea of low-sodium is. Always be prepared. Eat no airline food on the way to your contest. Wait until the return.

Wednesday should be your last workout before a Saturday show, but from the previous Sunday on, each workout should be progressively cut down in length. Make up for this by practicing the compulsories and your free posing routine two hours a day. Make sure they're full poses— that the whole body is posed and flexed. Just flexing your arms in an upper body pose is not good enough. Use that full-length mirror like never before. It's a work mirror, not an ego mirror. Go to it. Turn your focus inward. Force yourself to get *into* the whole thing; really into it. Sooner than you think, you'll be walking out on that stage. . . .

19

CONTEST-DAY
PREPARATION

When most people begin weight training their goals are modest. They'll think "I just want to add a little size to my chest and arms" or "I need to get rid of a couple of inches around my waist." Yet, when results come they're invariably driven to make more improvement. It's not long before friends notice the changes, and soon after, thoughts of competing arise.

When I first started competing I was very nervous, but my anxiety soon disappeared upon realizing I was being taken seriously. I credit my early success to regular, quality training and complete contest rehearsal. I've always been pretty thorough in my preparations for anything, always taken to heart the Boy Scouts' motto: "Be Prepared."

In body-building competition, much of your success, perhaps 95 percent of it, will be achieved before setting foot on stage. If you haven't put in the *rehearsal* time at the gym, and given adequate attention to nutrition and posing preparations, then you're not going to finish high in the standings. The following is a checklist of items you should take with you to a contest:

Three pairs of posing trunks. Pose trunks should conform to the standards of the day and should be designed to enhance your physical peculiarities (i.e., short-legged people could benefit from having very high-cut briefs). The reason for taking more than one pair is that your first pair could get oil on them backstage or at the pre-judging. Because pre-judging is so arduous, dark-color trunks are preferable since sweat and oil can cause color running and blotches.

Three music cassettes. Give one cassette of your posing music to a trusted friend or spouse. Keep two in your gym bag. Remember that without your music you're dead in the water, so guard it with your life. Your music should be recorded by itself at the beginning of both sides of all three tapes.

Two towels. You may break out into a sweat during your warm-up and need to dab face, neck, chest, etc., to prevent too much color run. Towels can also be used as a warm-up aid (lat pulls) or to cover the face while lying backstage to help meditation or relaxation. They're also necessary to remove oil after the competition. Few backstage areas have showers.

Brush or comb. A quick run through your hair with either a brush or comb may give you that additional clean-cut look that makes for an overall winning and athletic appearance.

Tube of coloring. Most pros who use or need skin coloring use Fast Tan or Dy-O-Derm. My final coat of color is Clinique bronzer. It's a good idea to take a small tube of your coloring for the odd touch-up should the situation require it.

Posing oil. Some use apricot or almond oil in the belief that it tightens the skin. I don't believe in this theory. I use Nivea skin oil and oil in cream. Make sure that the bottle of oil you take is placed in a sealed plastic bag in case of leakage.

Salt and potassium packs. Salt will act as a quick fix if you're cramping during pre-judging. You should take just enough, along with sips of water to take the edge off your cramps. You should have a few potassium tablets on hand, though, in the event you want to adjust your balance of body fluids.

Rubber thongs. These help keep your feet clean and should be worn at all times backstage. Most backstage areas are very unclean, and dirty feet will show up in several poses, mostly when the calves or hamstrings are being displayed.

Water. Include Evian-type water; not the distilled variety, which is nothing more that "dead" liquid. You need a nonsodium water, but at no time should you gulp it down in large quantities.

Meals. Take two preprepared "meals." Typically, these would include rice, baked potatoes or yams, and skinless chicken. Take along plenty of raisins and dried fruit to keep your glycogen level high. Keep eating in small amounts consistently through the day. To preserve freshness, these foods should be placed in plastic compartmentalized containers or sealed lock plastic bags.

Personal Walkman. Being backstage can be an anxious time for competitors. One can easily become agitated. My solution is to listen to my posing music two or three times, mentally rehearsing the routine in my mind's eye. At other times I may tune in to a guided meditation–type tape to induce relaxation.

Remember the psyching-out techniques brought to light by Arnold in the film _Pumping Iron_? Well, in truth, this type of thing doesn't happen too much at contests, at least not the pro contests I enter. If it does, I'm so tuned in to what I'm doing that I don't notice. All athletes are pretty wired before an event. It's natural to be uptight. My solution is to find an isolated area backstage where I can relax and turn my concentration inward, focusing on the matter at hand. I definitely don't believe in mind games. You should be composed prior to competition, not aggressive or agitated. Attempting to psyche out others doesn't work. It muddles the thinking process and causes edema, and the adrenals pump overtime because of the "fight or flight" syndrome you've precipitated—psyching games only show insecurity. You can be certain that if some arrogant body-builder tries to psyche you out, he's afraid of you. Don't even dignify his verbal abuse or sneers with a reply.

Backstage, you should keep your sweats on as long as possible. Keep warm. Even the mildest breeze or hint of coolness can cause your veins to shrivel to nothing.

To pump or not to pump, that is the question. I have been told on good authority that body-building stars of the fifties and sixties would sometimes go through a complete workout before going on stage. Personally, I don't believe in trying to pump up the muscles to an inflated size. For every fraction of an inch you add, there'll be a corresponding loss of hardness and muscle delineation. Remember the times in the gym when you got so pumped you couldn't flex a muscle? Well, you certainly don't need that now. Your homework should already be done.

Yes, warm up, pump a little, but restrict your activity to a couple of sets of thirty reps each. Prior to this, though, start by going through your compulsory poses in a quiet place. Begin by semi-tensing to warm up, then proceed to full contraction.

Now you're ready for your warm-up. Perform a combination of push-ups, towel pulls (with a partner), side raises with light dumbbells, or any of the "freehand" exercises shown in the buddy section, all to put an edge of blood into the muscle. As for the legs . . . only stretch and flex them. Too much blood in the legs is not good. If your front thighs are pumped, you won't be able to flex as thoroughly.

When the emcee's announcement calls you out to the stage, it can be a little unnerving, but you'll get used to it. In time you may even enjoy being on stage in competition.

After you're introduced to the audience, either individually or as a group (the lightweights, middleweights, etc.), you'll be asked to participate in the various rounds. Perform your poses as they're called. Don't wait around for the person next to you to start a pose before you hit your version. Posing and holding a position can be very exhausting. This is where your rehearsal time pays off. "Find" your poses according to my earlier guidelines, but then hold them like a statue until the head judge calls "Relax." Don't wildly twist and turn to give everyone in the auditorium a frontal view—just the opposite will happen. No one will get a front view; at least not for long enough to appreciate it. If the judges are situated in every direction, then pan them slowly, very slowly.

One of the most difficult things to face in big-time competition is *not* being chosen as an early call-out. There you are up on stage with twenty or more body-builders, and you're being overlooked. At times it seems everyone else is being called out to be compared: everyone but you. It can be humiliating and soul-destroying. Your mind plays tricks. For a brief second you even wonder if you haven't been called out because the judges have decided that you're so obviously *the best* on stage. Such is seldom the case, believe me!

So what to do? You hang tight, that's what. Keep erect, think positive. Hook those arms on your lats, keep your head up, your stomach pulled in, your thighs tight and your calves fanned. . . . Keep that look of confidence, because if you sulk and let your pride sag you'll place lower and lower, and you may never get called out at all. You have to look at contests as a way of measuring your improvement. Of course, you want to win, but you can't win them all. No one has an unbeaten streak. Even two of the greatest athletes in sport's history, Lee Haney and Arnold Schwarzenegger, have known defeat. They both used defeat to motivate them to even higher levels of achievement. A final word to serious contestants: Don't be a backstage jerk. Remember, you're an ambassador of body-building. Don't wipe your oily hands on the stage drapes. You could find that the $3000 cleaning bill is

sent to your address. Always try to act responsibly. At your next show you may emerge the winner, but if not, make it a point to congratulate the person who does win. Hold up his hand and smile, even if you don't agree with the decision. Keep your emotions and opinions to yourself—or for those private times when you're jawing with friends. When the pain of losing is at its peak, quietly resolve to come back better than ever *next* time. After all, neither Rome nor Paris was built in a day.

20

FLEX POSING

I learned something early on in body-building that became incredibly important as I began to set my sights on competition: I discovered that building a shapely, defined physique was not just a matter of pushing hard in workouts, juggling exercises and monitoring nutrition. It also involved *tensing* the muscles, finding the contraction and flexing them for short practice sessions on a regular basis. This is especially true for the competition aspirant. When you tense a muscle you get to know it better; you're learning to feel it, isolate it and ultimately control it. In time and with plenty of practice you find that this flexing does help improve shape, separation and even definition. For proof, just look at the amazing Tom Platz in his heyday. As part of Tom's routine he performed his signature *abdominals and thigh* pose (sometimes known as the "hair" pose, because he accompanied it with a mock gesture of running his hands through his hair). Tom began by crunching down with his abs and then, with his right leg extended, bounce-flexing his quads to the max. Not only were his thighs huge, but when he tensed there was a mass of separation and amazing cross-striations that invariably brought the audience to loud cheers and unabashed, foot-stomping applause. It was when I noticed that Tom could only bring about this magic with his right leg that I learned the vital importance that flexing (Joe Weider calls it "isotension") plays in the development of muscular quad. Platz, by favoring his right leg in quad displays, had carved in extra maturity (definition, separation, cross-striations) that he was unable to duplicate in his left leg. You can be sure that no other factor was responsible. Tom likes to cycle, run and perform leg extensions, leg curls and squats, but at no time during these activities did he favor one leg over the other. No sir, it was his constant right thigh flexing that made the difference.

I'll give you another example. Samir Bannout, the 1983 Mr. Olympia and one of the *real* enthusiasts of our sport, loves to flex his muscles. It keeps him in tune with his body. He seldom lets go of his mind-muscle link and, accordingly, never loses touch with any body part. In fact, heaven help you if you're a long-lost friend of Samir's, and happen to meet him in a public place. Chances are, whether you're in a gym or a grocery store, Samir's pants will be down around his ankles and he'll be flashing his amazing quads to show you his latest progress. This enthusiasm, genuine love of body-building and ever-readiness to flex and pose for his fans has kept him tight and shapely. There are many iron men out there who train more aggressively than Samir, but few even begin to approach his muscular "finish," which is impressive even in the off-season. I believe that the high quality of his physique can be at least partly credited to his habit of flexing throughout the day.

It's not in my nature to flex and pose for friends or gym members, but because I see a very real value in flexing to gain an extra edge in competition, I've formed a basic *muscle-flexing* plan to increase the visual effectiveness of the seven compulsory poses. I follow this routine prior to an important competition.

You should start by setting regular time aside each day twelve weeks before the contest date. You're going to adopt each compulsory pose and hold the position I describe for ten to fifteen seconds. Use a full-length mirror. Don't just practice upper body poses. You're learning to look your best from head to toe; that's how the judges see you. You're up there in front of a dozen or so judges, virtually naked, being scrutinized for physical imperfections by the most knowledgeable people in the sport. It's easy to be intimidated, so that's why I'm taking you through each pose myself. In that way you'll be as prepared as anyone can be.

The back poses can only be seen properly if you have a second full-length mirror situated behind you. By positioning the two mirrors carefully you'll be able to view your body from every angle. After all, the judges will be viewing you from all angles....

Once you've "set" each pose, flex all your visible muscles in such a way that you look your most impressive. Don't suddenly pop a forced smile at the judging panel. Allow your smile to come naturally. If you're in shape, you'll be looking and feeling so good that a natural smile will creep across your face regardless. Above all, remember that not only is your physique improved by posing practice, but the poses themselves fall into place far more dramatically if they've been steadily practiced throughout your body-building career. It's never too early to start. In the order they would be called out onstage, here are the compulsory poses. Practice them according to my suggestions (important note—in every single pose you're showing the entire body from head to toe; for example, a double biceps is not just an arm pose, it's also a calf, leg, ab, chest, etc., pose).

FRONT DOUBLE BICEPS

This is one of the most telling of all poses. Not only are you showing your entire torso and lats (from the front), but you also have to coordinate the difficult task of flexing the legs and the arms at the same time. The *double biceps* is also a silhouette pose. This is to say, your overall outline shape is being judged as well as your various individual muscle areas.

- Keep your shoulders down throughout the pose.
- Raise your elbows slightly higher than your shoulders to enhance the overall flowing line. Upper arms parallel to the floor is not recommended.
- Endeavor to stretch out lats and ''lock in'' on serratus.
- Lift rib cage, but not to the extent that you're sucking in the entire midsection— find a middle path where you

Front Double Biceps

can show your abdominals while at the same time lifting your rib cage. Only a very few body-builders (like Lee Labrada) can crunch down their abdominals in this pose, and still look good. I don't recommend it for most athletes.

• Relax face and neck while concentrating on a total body flex.

FRONT LAT SPREAD

Unlike the front double-biceps pose, in which you have to get the lats to spread outward on their own, in this pose you can help things along by anchoring your hands at your midsection. Beginners often think that it's just a matter of pushing the fist against the hips until the lats spread outwards. Not so; in fact, very little pressure is applied by the hands.

• Begin from legs up. Set the legs, heels comfortably apart, but not in any way set wide.
• Place your closed fist above your hipbone, hooking the thumb around at the back to secure the position.
• Keep the shoulders down, but not so low as to bring the traps into play.
• Lift the rib cage while sucking in the waist and tensing the frontal abdominal wall.
• Don't lean backwards. This is especially important when being judged, because the likelihood is that the judges will be looking up at you and if you lean backwards the entire effect of your pose is lost.

__Front Lat Spread__

SIDE CHEST

Many body-builders make the mistake of just involving the upper body when practicing this pose. Keep in mind that it is, like the others, a full head-to-toe display. You should practice this pose from both sides, so that you look equally good in both positions.

- Picture yourself standing in a box. One side faces the audience, one side stage right, one side stage left. Keep the front of your body facing the audience and turn diagonally to face the rear corner.
- Lift the rib cage, pulling back on the elbow.
- Keep the near-side pec relaxed. Do not flex, roll, split or bounce it.
- Tense (split) the far-side pec and hold it tight for the duration of the pose.
- Place the front-leg toe into the instep of the straight (back) leg. Flex the calf.
- Work to find where the leg biceps looks impressive. Chances are it will look best when the leg biceps is relaxed and the glute is flexed.
- Raise one toe so that the knee and ankle are perfectly in line over each other. Side thigh cuts often take care of themselves, but keep the legs close together throughout.

Side Chest

REAR DOUBLE BICEPS

On the surface this pose is similar to the front double-biceps pose previously described. The difference is that you're displaying your back and not your front. This entails tensing the back muscles instead of the frontal areas, and leaning back slightly so that the judges will view you at the correct angle.

Start with the focus on the legs; place one leg back and flex the calf muscle.

Raise your arms as though you're going to do a lat pulldown. Pull downwards, open up the shoulders, raise the rib cage and spread the lats wide—turn arms back so that the judges can see them full on (not just the underside of your triceps).

When onstage you can turn your head slightly to the side, keeping your face relaxed at all times. This head movement serves to bring the judges' eyes back to your physique, because you're adding movement to a static position.

Rear Double Biceps

REAR LAT SPREAD

Again, at first this may seem to be an identical position to the front lat spread, but such is not the case. Instead of tensing the serratus, frontal abdominal fascia, and thighs, you're endeavoring to show back mass and width, plus hamstrings and rear calf muscles. Place one leg back and tense the calf. Round your shoulders with your hands above your hipbones, and stretch out. You need the double mirror now, more than ever, because you have to stretch out the back, maximizing the V taper, yet stopping to stretch before the back appears bowed. There is a point where the back V shape and the mass of the entire back look their best. Work with your mirror to find this ideal position. To stretch solely for maximum width invites the possibility of losing back detail (muscularity).

Again, because back poses seldom hold the judges' attention long, you can turn your head to one side after a few seconds to bring their view to *your* back. It works.

Rear Double Biceps

SIDE TRICEPS

Practice this pose from both sides; you never know when you may need to blow another competitor away by adopting an identical pose. But don't do it if there's any doubt in your mind; the opposite could happen. Again, as with the side chest pose, use the box technique. The front is facing the audience. The sides are stage left and stage right, remember? Hook your hands around your showing arm (nearest to the audience). Now twist the shoulders diagonally to the rear corner of the imaginary "box." Flex the triceps, but don't splay them out by pressing against the body—use your mirror to find the perfect flex position. Keep your stomach in. Blow air out, flex your intercostals, lift your rib cage slightly. Attempt to bring out the shoulder striations but don't roll them around or play them out. Press out against your hand (like the beginning of a side raise) to bring the separation out. "Set" your muscles like a marble statue and hold the position tight.

Side Triceps

ABDOMINALS AND THIGHS

Stand with one leg extended, knees slightly bent.   Act as though you're raising the front foot off the ground, but don't. This will flex the frontal thigh muscles to advantage. Remember to also flex the back leg. Place both hands behind the head, elbows up, face relaxed, shoulders down in the natural position. Blow out all the air and flex down on the abs. Experiment at home with both legs, and on the day of the contest go with the strongest leg—like Tom Platz, remember?

The position of the light is very important with this pose. Abdominals don't show up well if the lights are not hitting them strongly. On the day of the contest, when you flex down, take a quick glance to check that the light is still hitting the abdominals effectively.

__Abdominals__ __and__ __Thighs__

RELAXED FRONT POSITION

Actually, this pose is anything but relaxed—every muscle has to be tight. Always keep your body upright. Lift the rib cage slightly. Adopt a semi-lat spread in which the arms are "hooked" onto the lats but the position is not exaggerated—keep your head up. Flex the abs, but don't crunch down. Spread (fan) the calves and flex the thighs.... This can be exhausting, so the day of the contest you'll appreciate every moment of practice you allocated to this position. You must keep your thighs flexed the entire time onstage.

Relaxed Front Position

RELAXED POSITION FROM REAR

You have to show a strong V shape, yet not so much that the back thickness is lost. Experiment with various techniques to make the calves look their best. Some body-builders like to fan their calf out to maximize size, while others "grab" the floor with their toes and make their lower leg tendons "boil." Personally, I get the best effect from starting a calf raise, but not going up with the heels from the floor.

Relaxed Position from Rear

RELAXED POSITION FROM SIDE

One can't be too creative in this position. It would be nice to be able to dramatically twist the upper torso toward the judges' direction, but this is no longer allowed. Having said that, though, I believe a slight twist is both advantageous and allowed. Don't make the mistake of standing in the same way that you would in the front or back relaxed positions; remember, your triceps muscles are being viewed, not your lat spread. Tighten the triceps—keep your hand in the relaxed position; no fists, even though your entire *showing arm* will be tensed. Keep that head up, and facing straight ahead.

Relaxed Position from Side

Every four days add one more "round," until you are going through the compulsory poses fifteen times. Hold each position for ten to fifteen seconds, flexing from head to toe. Don't favor one part of the body at the expense of another.

Four to five weeks before your competition you must start practicing without the mirror. Remember, you have no mirror on stage.

Begin by performing one or two rounds of the compulsories with your eyes open (using the mirror), then start to hit poses with the eyes closed. After ten seconds open the eyes and make adjustments. You're aiming for that perfect position that needs no correction. When your eyes are closed, ask yourself about the pose: Is it right? Is your head in the right position? Are your feet placed correctly? Are the abs flexed? Are you grimacing? Is your neck too stressed? Are you belly-breathing? Every pose should have a *check system*.

Being onstage is going to be difficult. It's never a breeze. A prejudging is harder than your hardest workout. Those of you who have rehearsed it will make it look easy, but it's hard. Be prepared.

21

THE ART OF PRESENTATION

Perhaps the most artistic aspect of body-building is the free-posing round. It's also the least understood, even by professional body-builders. The administrators of the sport continue to send conflicting signals. They give lip service to the need for creative posing, but the day of the contest, creativity often doesn't seem to count for much. It's very confusing. I see posing as a theatrical display, and in recent years that side of it has grown and matured for me. I'm telling a story with the movement and positioning of my body. I still insert plenty of double biceps, side chests, and even lat spreads and most musculars, but I connect them with a variety of transformations and lead-ins. I try to always be innovative with my posing, and it's brought me both acclaim and criticism. Many, especially those who favor artistic posing, feel that I'm the greatest body-building poser in the world, while others feel that anything I do that isn't a conventional, time-accepted, hard-core pose is a waste of time.

As a professional, my natural sense of performance forbids me from executing the same posing routine too often. I usually change it completely every contest phase. For the major contest that typically begins the grand prix circuit, I'll have a new routine, and I'll keep to this routine for the smaller grand prix that follow during the year. But for the next major contest, usually the following year, I'll have another routine. I suppose I do this more for the fans and for my own satisfaction than to gain points in competition, because several of the body-builders who have won most often have hardly changed their routines over the last ten years, and their lack of innovation hasn't hurt them a bit.

In my earlier amateur days I used graceful transitions between my poses (this type of presentation is now considered the best posing style). In time, though, I felt a need to move beyond that—to develop a more innovative presentation. After all, the sport doesn't grow unless you attempt to do something different....

Posing must be entertaining, and why not? You should attempt to hold people on the edge of their seats with what you're doing. I'm not a big believer in going out, hitting most musculars and nodding to the crowd, soliciting applause. I don't seek applause *during* my posing; I want people to be engrossed—with their mouths open—throughout the whole thing. Even in my early days of competition, at the Mr. Los Angeles, I would never hear much clapping during my routine. It would always be afterwards, and frequently I got more than anyone else. Since those days it's always been a goal of mine to have the audience on the edge of their seats, enthralled with the performance, rather than applauding every pose during the exhibition. When you're performing a free-posing routine you have to think of the overall picture, to concentrate on the movement and the flow as well as the individual poses.

Posing has to be done to music, and the choice of music must *work* with your selected routine. Nothing frustrates me more than sitting in the audience at a show and seeing someone use a wonderful piece and yet fail to interpret it in any way. It's almost as if there are two movies playing. Invariably, the more beautiful the music, the more gruesome the poser. (You know, really moving music and you have this Neanderthal up there contorting, grunting, huffing and puffing, totally out of sync with anything that's happening on the stereo system.) When this happens I often find myself daydreaming, wondering what I could do with the same music. I think that many body-builders, especially the hard-core "bulkers," feel it's unmasculine to interpret the music with any sensitivity. In fact, the opposite is true.

Over the years I've used several pieces of music successfully. I was the first body-builder to use the theme from *Chariots of Fire*. A week after the movie came out I had a contest, so I rushed up to the music store and put a routine together for the music. Shortly afterwards, everyone started using it. In the early eighties I used Jean Michel Jaret's *Equinoxe* and the theme from *The Natural*. I think a lot of people have seen me pose to that in the videos from my early Mr. Olympias. Recently, I've used—and I'm really having a good time posing to—female ballad singers such as Tracy Chapman, Cher, and Jennifer Rush. But I don't rule out any type of music—it simply must be effective. When choosing posing music, listen to the rhythm. Ask yourself, "How can I move to that rhythm?" Remember that, though you may have an affection for hard rock, the audience may not share that enthusiasm when it accompanies your routine on stage. Could prove embarrassing....

Neophyte posers have to start slowly. If you haven't flexed a muscle before, you'll probably have difficulty tensing a thigh and a biceps at the same time. So how do you go about acquiring good poses for yourself? First, check out the muscle magazines, study the various videos and attend local contests, so you build up an accurate picture of what posing is all about. Don't be overanxious to copy the top title winners. Quite often, they're successful in spite of their posing ability, not because of it. It's like learning to swing a golf club: You study the style of a professional who's noted as a stylist, whose swing is technically perfect. Forget the pro whose swing breaks every rule in the book (even though he may be a big money winner on the pro circuit). Similarly, look to body-builders who've proven over time that they're excellent posers—people like Cory Everson, Mohamed Makkawy, Tonya Knight, Lee Labrada and Anja Langer. These people pose with fluidity, grace and drama, and they still hold on to the essential core of physique display: showing off the muscular body to advantage.

When you first start to pose, ten-to-one it will be a flexed biceps in the bathroom mirror. Okay, you're on your way. After this initial self-inspection, it's a good idea to get acquainted with the compulsory poses. Let's take a look at how to build an acceptable double biceps pose. Concentrate first on placing your feet; then think about the angle of your calves; now consider the direction of your knees; flex the frontal thigh; now the direction of the hips. . . . Your goal is to create an illusion. That is to say, you want your shoulders and upper back to look wide while at the same time minimalizing the visual width of your hip and waist areas. In body-building competition it's not enough to be big and muscular—you also need to pose cleverly, to make some areas appear larger than life while keeping other parts in the background. In spite of his massive upper body and huge limbs, Arnold Schwarzenegger would still twist his body dramatically in most frontal poses. He wanted to exaggerate in an attempt to change people's perceptions from "totally built" to "utterly unbelievable."

Think in terms of creating an illusion with all your poses, whether they're from the side, front or back. Let's go back to that box on the floor once again. How can you twist your shoulders, for example, if you are standing to the side? Well, the hips will look smallest from an audience (frontal) point of view if you place the flat front part of the hip against that side of the box. And the shoulders are going to look their widest when you turn them diagonally, toward the corner of the box.

The visually impressive points (reference points that are usually looked at first) are the shoulders, waist and calves, so you want to accentuate the impressiveness of these areas as much as possible. Beware of hunching your shoulders up around your neck in your poses. It may seem natural, but it doesn't look right. Keep them down and practice your posing over and over. This is your rehearsal time to ensure future competence. Put in enough thought and practice and you may even exceed your wildest hopes. The more you pose the better you'll be able to control your muscles, and the better they will look.

One of the most interesting segments of a physique competition is the *posedown*. That's where the top six contestants are allowed to perform any poses they want in order to gain an edge over their competitors. I've seen some pretty tame posedowns in my time, but most I've competed in have been little short of physical mayhem. The pros usually refrain from actual shoving and pushing, but you can expect the occasional elbow in the ribs because competitors seem to angle for the stage-center spot, which can get pretty crowded. I myself don't seek out people to invade their space, but I don't run away either. Some people function best pushing right into the ground and trying by sheer force to grab the judges' eyes. It depends on your personal style. Generally, judges are looking for hardness. The posedown is the time to show them what you've got. This translates to "most musculars" galore. Everyone's done them, so in order to compete in this final round you have to join the crowd and follow suit. This doesn't mean that you can't throw in your signature pose, or something that shows head-to-foot proportion. Truthfully, though, your best Joe Weider pose (arms folded, three-quarter front) would probably be wasted. You should show that hardness and keep it coming by repeating many of your most impressive positions. And don't hold your poses for more than a few seconds. The posedown is grueling; keep them coming fast and furious. If you feel you don't have a chance to win, you can stop when the head judge calls "halt." But if you smell victory, then keep posing until they drag you off the stage!

Since I've spent most of my body-building life developing superior balance, I'm always upset when I see a big title awarded to someone whose balance is way out of line. And it's not just because I happen to have

balance. I can remember seeing pictures of disproportionately built body-builders *before* I'd built my own body. A twenty-one-inch arm does not go with a fifteen-inch calf! It defies every law of aesthetics.

Judging today is based on how muscular and hard a body-builder is. All rounds are judged this way. In spite of naming them the symmetry round, the muscularity round, the posing round, etc., they're all judged by a single criterion . . . muscular *hardness*. Accordingly, when a perfectly built person is up on stage showing proportion, symmetry, muscularity,

mass and definition, all put together with faultless presentation, he can be cast from the winner's circle by some "mountain of muscle" who with *lat spreads* and *most musculars* bullies the judges into giving him first place. It's wrong. The thinking is wrong. Okay, so the name of the game is body-*building*. Fine. We can't have some ninety-four-pound weakling coming in, however ripped and proportioned, and winning over a well-proportioned *built* physique. But more sound and sensible judgment in assessing a body-builder's physique is needed to bring things back into perspective.

Sometimes I fantasize about having seven areas of judging: muscularity, symmetry, shape, proportion, size, definition and presentation. Judges could use a 1–10 rating system, including fractions similar to the Olympic diving and ice-skating scoring systems (e.g., 7.5 could be awarded in a category). In this way the judges' attention would be specifically directed toward these categories, which up till now have been left up to the individual judge to either consider or entirely ignore. (Regrettably, there are judges out there who don't choose to award additional "points" for good shape or proportion, or even for presentation.)

Happily, there's evidence that things are changing. The well-proportioned physique seems to be climbing the ladder of recognition. The winds of change are long overdue.

Appendix A

QUESTIONS AND ANSWERS

Q. I've recently joined a gym that has a large number of exercise machines. Most are totally new to me. Should I keep using free weights or go with the machines?

A. You should follow a basic free-weight program, incorporating the accepted machines such as leg extensions, calf machines, leg press machines, cable crossovers and lat machines.

On an experimental basis, though, you should gradually bring each machine into your realm of experience. You may need to use a machine a dozen times to be able to make a judgment; it depends on your degree of experience. Most top body-builders can tell after one set whether a machine has merit or not. Gradually, you'll learn which machines suit your particular needs and you can then make a decision to use them as part of your armory of exercises or discard them entirely.

Q. I've see pictures of body-builders who have ugly stretch marks at the side of the pectorals. How can I avoid getting these? Are they curable?

A. The best cure is prevention. Follow a program of sound nutrition. I had minor stretch marks at the beginning of my body-building career, due to poor eating habits. People who have them should try to prevent their spread by applying vitamin E cream to keep the skin elastic and moisturized. The key, however, is to not push yourself to gain too much mass in a short period of time. If you've recently developed stretch marks (and they're still red), see your doctor. There are new creams available that can fade them considerably. If they've already turned brown, then nothing short of surgery will remove them.

Q. I'm excessively thin right now at twenty-eight years of age. I don't want to have a huge Mr. Universe body, but I do want to be well built. Are there special techniques I should be using?

A. No. Whether you want to build a fit, toned and proportionate body or one of Mr. Olympia standards, there's very little difference in training technique. The difference is in commitment and time devoted to the task.

Both the decathlon athlete and the gymnast employ a huge amount of variety in their training. Translated to your progressive resistance workouts, this means that multi-angular training is the secret to looking good from all angles.

Q. I'm fourteen years old and would like to start weight training. Is there an optimum age to begin?

A. I don't believe *very* young kids should train past normal failure. Moderate, sensible body-building that doesn't involve excessive strain or poor exercise style is fine for healthy youngsters, but usually their attention span is lacking. Kids prefer to play sports rather than involve themselves in the discipline of formal weight training.

Excessive strain is not recommended for youngsters, because their tendons, ligaments and bone structure are still going through the growth process. I don't see why teenagers shouldn't be encouraged to take up body-building if they have the interest, but they need to be careful they don't burn out. Many do. Concentrate on improving your physique, but don't let the temptation of becoming a great teenage body-builder undermine your long-term goals. If your goal is to become a competitor in the Mr. Olympia when you're an adult, and you're realistic about that goal, then think about your short-term goals. Think about the possibility that you can easily burn out your body at a young age. For the noncompetitive teenage athlete...the most important thing is to work for the *feel* of the muscle, finding the contraction and looking for balance in the physique.

Q. I've heard conflicting arguments about wearing a belt. Some people say you should wear a belt to protect the back. Others say a belt is like a crutch, and that wearing it will only weaken the body and make it more susceptible to injury. What's your opinion?

A. A belt should be used as a tool, not a crutch. I've seen many body-builders wear a belt throughout their workout. A belt can be necessary for those exercises that put stress on the lower back, but I think you should do without a belt if you can. A belt is most useful as a support when doing heavy squats. It protects the back and permits you to brace the body against the belt, which has a positive effect on the lift. (Never use a belt on the leg-curl machine, by the way. The buckle could tear the vinyl covering.)

Q. Does a physique need vascularity (a veiny appearance) to look good? If so, how can I obtain it?

A. Vascularity is a sign of thin skin, which in itself is an indication that you're holding a low body-fat percentage. No body—male or female—looks good with excess fat, so it follows that most good-looking physiques have some vascularity.

I personally don't like the appearance of pop-up vascularity all over the body. It interferes with the separation line of the muscles—you don't see what's going on. It's as though you put the veins on an overlay and when you lift it off, there's not quite the super physique you imagined underneath. In physique competition it's confusing to judges, too. When the audience sees veins popping up it "oohs and aahs." And the judges, who're similarly affected, score the individual higher. In truth, vascularity has nothing to do with the muscle size and shape.

Vascularity comes about from years of routinely exercising muscles to their fullest pump. Mature, well-trained muscle areas often have a pleasant-looking vascularity. For years, I didn't have any vascularity in my frontal thigh, because my skin was a little thicker in this area, but with the maturity of the body part, I now have skin so thin, most of the time, and a capillary system so developed that my legs show considerable vascularity.

Nice clean veins running through the legs or arms enhance the physique.

Q. What's your position on knee wraps? Are they a help to the body-builder who just wants to shape up, or should they only be worn by an advanced body-builder training for competition?

A. The first time I wrapped my knees I'd been doing 315 pounds of moderate reps, and I immediately was able to squat with 405 for the same number of reps. Using wraps tends to be a security thing, like wearing a seat belt. You can drive a little faster, knowing that if things get out of hand, you have some protection. A wrap shouldn't be done up tight. It should only be used for knee support and, in my opinion, shouldn't be used by beginners. You have to pay your squatting dues by working your legs without any support for at least two years. Then, when you've earned the right to use wraps (because you're at the point where the poundage you're using puts you at risk of severe injury), you can place them on. Wrap below and above the knee—alternate one turn above the knee cap and then one turn below the knee cap. Pop off the wraps between sets for comfort and to allow the blood to flow freely.

Q. Can you give me your opinion on training partners? Are they necessary if you just want good muscle tone and not a gargantuan physique? Also, can a strong athlete train successfully with a much weaker athlete?

A. You'd be surprised at how many top body-builders go through their workouts alone. Generally, though, if a contest date is looming, it's advisable for a competitive body-builder to train with a workout partner.

If your body-building goals are more modest, a training partner is not needed, except perhaps to spot you on benches and squats. You *would* make faster progress using a partner. But it has to be the right person.

You want someone with the same commitment to performance— someone who can help motivate you through the workout. A training partnership is a two-way street. You should use small words of encouragement, spoken softly—"Come on . . . one more rep . . . push through." You should remind each other to squeeze the weight. And at the conclusion of a well-fought set, add, "Good . . . great set."

Personally, I don't think a set should be turned into a big production. A training partnership should be almost quiet. There should be as much unspoken communication as spoken. And if this compatibility is lost or goals change, then it may be time to change your partner.

Yes, a strong athlete can train successfully with a much weaker one, but two pieces of apparatus must be used on the heavier lifts (if free weights are being used rather than selectorized machines). There's also no reason why a man and a woman can't work out well together.

Q. When is the ideal time to train? I've heard that early morning is best, but I feel pretty weak first thing. It takes me several hours to even feel energetic.

A. The time you train is not important. What is important is that you *do* train. Those with jobs or other commitments may not have much choice concerning what time they train.

If you're into tranquillity and solitude, then early-morning training may be ideal for you. Tom Platz thrived on training very early in the morning.

I happen to be a night person; accordingly, some of my best workouts have been late in the evening. The body likes to set its biological clock to ready itself for certain activities, so there's an advantage to training at approximately the same time each day. In fact, this is essential for the competitive body-builder training for a contest.

Q. How often should I take my measurements? I'd like to put at least five inches on my arms and ten inches on my chest. (What, by the way, are your measurements?)

A. I never take my own measurements, because to do so could conflict with the importance of building a physique that looks right, rather than one that measures right. The only statistics I know about my own body are that I'm six feet tall and weigh 240 pounds.

I suggest you forget about the tape measure and, rather than train for inches, train for a proportionate appearance. Make a biweekly mirror analysis of your entire physique and use your journal to tailor exercises to your immediate needs.

Q. What exercises do you consider totally useless?

A. This is a loaded question, because there's always someone who swears he gets super results from a particular exercise everyone else claims is a poor result-getter.

My approach is to be cautiously optimistic about most exercises. Bring them into your realm of experience—check them out for yourself before discarding them completely. I will stick my neck out and say that ballistic-type movements could be risky. Never invite trouble by bouncing your squats, deadlifts or bench presses or by turning any free-weight exercise into a ballistic movement.

I also don't like the weighted side bend (holding a heavy dumbbell in one hand and performing side bends). This will only lead to heavy oblique development and a wider waistline area. I'm not convinced, either, about the value of straight arm pullovers. Finally, although bent-over rowing is a good lat-thickening exercise, you should be very careful when using excessive weight. In this movement the back is put in a precarious position, and unless care is taken an injured lower back could result.

Because body-builders tend to be heavier than most athletes, I'm not in favor of distance running. The knees and feet could be permanently injured from the pounding action. It's far better to keep the pressure on the leg's muscles, through, for example, stationary bike riding or power walking (where jerking is minimized).

Q. I've often wondered if body-building changes the bone structure in any way. Can you give me your thoughts on this?

A. It's a scientific fact that bones tend to strengthen with regular weight training. This is especially true of older people whose bones may become more brittle and weak with lack of use. Our bones also tend to grow to accommodate added body weight, whether it be muscle or fat. Have you noticed how the skeletal appearance of people who've just lost a large amount of weight seems expanded? Rib cages seem bigger, shoulders wider. If these same people hold a low body weight for a prolonged period of time, the skeletal structure will start to diminish slightly, but it may never quite return to its pre-training size.

When I stopped heavy training to enroll in acting school in the mid-eighties, I deliberately took my body weight down from 245 to 195. I kept fit with various circuit and cross-training methods, but I did no heavy body-building for two years or so. When I lost the weight, I noticed that my frame had changed somewhat to accommodate my previously held muscle mass. (I actually felt wide-hipped, because even though my hips were about forty inches in circumference at both body weights, my shoulder and lat mass had been reduced. In actual fact, of course, they were merely normal. The same thing happened regarding my knee and ankle joints; without my huge quads and calves, the bones appeared quite sturdy, yet when I'm up in muscular body weight these same bony areas appear quite small.)

Q. I noticed you training in World Gym not long ago and was impressed by your posture. Whether you were performing seated curls or squats or just loading weight on a bar, your posture (from every angle) always seemed remarkably correct. What's your secret?

A. Good posture has to come naturally—it can't be forced. If you have a rounded back or incorrectly aligned shoulders or hips, you can't just haul yourself up with a single correcting adjustment and leave it at that. Good posture results from balanced exercise, pride of deportment and faultless joint alignment.

First, don't fall into the habit of adopting a lazy posture; you'll grow into the shape that you assume most frequently. That's why people who read, write or type incorrectly often develop rounded backs. Long-distance cyclists, for example, invariably develop a permanently rounded upper back. I see many postural defects. One of the major ones is holding one shoulder higher than the other. When you're using your *work mirror* whether you're a body-building competitor or not, look at your general appearance and study your joints, your key points (such as the shoulders and waist) and how you're holding your hips. Ask yourself if you have problems with your alignments. Make a conscious effort to level up your shoulders, or straighten your back...everything from head to tailbone should be in straight alignment.

Good posture doesn't just improve your appearance, it also helps the health of the spine. If you have a severe problem with your posture, consult a qualified chiropractor. You may be in need of a tailor-made correctional program.

Q. I've just started to compete and have noticed that competitors today have highly developed buttocks. Is this development necessary for me to be successful?

A. Your observation that all the competitors today seem to have developed buttocks is accurate. Actually, body-builders refer to the buttocks as the *glutes,* and their development is essential for a complete physique.

Of course, there's a fine line between development and overdevelopment. The muscular area that stretches from the lower back to the top of the hamstrings *must* be developed in proportion with the rest of the physique. Meeting that goal will mean taking diet into consideration. Both men and women have a tendency to store a high level of fat in the glute area. You'll need to be very disciplined with your nutrition in order to push beyond ordinary low-fat levels.

Muscle development takes place in two ways, directly and indirectly. Indirect glute development results from leg exercises such as squats, leg presses, lunges and leg curls. Low-back exercises such as hyperextensions and stiff-leg deadlifts also hit the glutes indirectly. Of these exercises, squats exert the greatest stress on the glutes. So as long as your knees and lower back are in good shape, squatting is a key exercise, not only for front thigh development but also for complete glute development.

In my armory of exercises, I include two direct glute exercises. The focus of both movements is to isolate the muscle. The first movement I call the *glute crunch.* Lying on your back with your knees bent and feet flat on the floor, begin the movement with your hips resting on the ground. The motion of this movement will be to raise your hips toward the ceiling, keeping your feet, upper back, shoulders and head resting on the ground. If the movement doesn't put stress on your lower back, keep the back arched upwards slightly. If it causes discomfort, do the exercise with less arch to the back. As with all exercises, contraction is the key. You'll want to raise your hips as high as they will go and clench your glute muscles at the top. Hold the contraction for a beat and repeat the movement. You can alter your foot positions to affect different areas of the muscle.

The second direct exercise is a one-leg kickback using a low pulley machine. For this movement you'll need a bench, adjustable ankle straps (that will enable you to hook your leg to the pulley machine) and a low pulley machine. This exercise can also be done without a machine, using only the weight of your leg, but you'll get greater resistance and results using a moderate weight and medium-high to high reps (twenty to fifty). Attach one leg to the low pulley and rest on the opposite knee on a bench placed in front of the pulley. Rest your hands in front of you on the bench or on the floor, wherever you can best find your balance.

Beginning with the leg that's attached by the ankle to the pulley machine, bend your knee forward and raise it up under the chest. Using a smooth movement, push back and up with the leg until it extends directly out behind you. The leg when extended should be just above parallel to the ground. Flex your glute muscle at the top of the movement. Do your reps and switch legs so you give equal attention to both sides. I work my glutes on leg days because of the indirect work involved. I end my workout by using two or three sets of both direct glute exercises mentioned above, doing between twenty and fifty repetitions per set.

Using these direct and indirect movements, combined with balanced, clean nutrition, will create well-developed, fat-free glutes for competition or the beach.

Q. I'm new to body-building workouts, and I have noticed that some people in the gym use straps for certain exercises. Can you tell me if they're necessary, and if so, what their purpose is?

A. Whether you use training straps or not is entirely up to you. The purpose in using straps is to secure your grip in exercises where the grip is likely to give out before the muscle being worked does. Straps were developed originally by weight lifters who worked at the regular deadlift exercise to supplement their strength. At the time, the deadlift was considered the only exercise where the grip could give out before the muscles.

When body-builders started increasing intensity in the early 1980s (by using heavier weights and higher reps and going to positive failure), straps took on a new popularity. Today they're used in bent-over rowing, deadlifts, pull-ups, shrugs, upright rows and pulldowns—in fact, in any exercise where the bar is pulling away from

One-Leg _Low_ _Pulley_ _Kickback_ (start)

One-Leg _Low_ _Pulley_ _Kickback_ (finish)

your grip. (One wouldn't use training straps for exercises like squats, bench presses or flyes.) I use straps in certain exercises, because I believe in using any aid that will help me maximally stimulate my muscles.

Q. I'm a competitive body-builder who wants his picture accepted by one of the muscle magazines. How do I go about this? I've won several local contests.

A. There are many body-builders in your category. Very few get much publicity, because they put a camera into an amateur's hands and perform a most muscular pose in their backyard. The problems are predictable:

1. Picture out-of-focus and blurry
2. A cluttered, distracting background
3. An uneven tan
4. Too much strain on face
5. Unkempt hair
6. No oil on body
7. Sun too high in the sky
8. Too much fat on the body
9. An inappropriate or awkward pose
10. Poor choice of trunks and outer clothing

Put yourself in a magazine editor's position. Every day the mail brings pictures of known and unknown body-builders. All want publicity. But ask yourself: How can an editor use a single, out-of-focus picture of someone performing a most muscular pose in some cluttered backyard? It's not a news item, is it? You didn't march down New York's Fifth Avenue turning over cabs with your mighty strength, did you? So the picture would have to be run based on its own merits (i.e., *your* muscles). Unfortunately, if the focus of the picture is soft, the background cluttered and the clothing inappropriate, the only chance of publication the picture has is if you're outrageously built or perfectly proportioned from head to toe—built to such an extent that the technically poor aspects of the picture can be forgiven. This is a very rare occurrence.

Generally, magazine editors are not interested in a single picture. They want a package. That is, they're looking for new faces, yes, but they want to introduce up-and-coming body-builders to their readers via a biographical article (including training and diet information) that is submitted with *realistic* training and physique photos. Before you seek publicity, make sure you're at the point where you're happy with the way you look. Don't fool yourself. If you built only the frame and axles of a car, you wouldn't take it to the auto show. Make sure you're pretty much complete before you go blowing your horn.

• • • • •

MY LISTS OF FAVORITES

• • • • •

Ten Favorite Body-Builders

1. Arnold Schwarzenegger
2. Lee Haney
3. Cory Everson
4. Lee Labrada
5. Berry DeMay
6. Robby Robinson
7. Frank Zane
8. Bev Francis
9. Carla Dunlap
10. Diana Dennis

Ten Favorite Gyms in the World

1. World Gym, Venice, California
2. Fitness School, Michael Scherz, Sandhausen, West Germany

3. Muscle & Fitness Camp Gym, Los Angeles, California
4. Fassi Forma, Zingonia, Italy
5. Wag Bennets Gym, London, England
6. Broadway Bodyworks, Denver, Colorado
7. Weider Gym, Paris, France
8. Muscle Machine, Birmingham, England
9. World Gym, Manhattan, New York
10. Top Body, Vienna, Austria

Ten Favorite Exercises

1. Back squat
2. Half-deadlift/shrug
3. Triceps pushdown
4. Lying leg curl
5. Incline dumbbell curl
6. Dips
7. Low pulley rows
8. Lying side raise dumbbell
9. Lunges
10. Incline press

Ten Favorite Exercise Techniques

1. Down the rack
2. Tri-sets
3. Very-high-rep leg work
4. Bi-sets
5. Peak contraction
6. Super sets
7. Rest days
8. Holding contractions
9. Stretching
10. Full movements

Ten Favorite Clean Foods

1. Oatmeal
2. Round steak
3. Rice
4. Red potatoes
5. Eggs
6. Bananas
7. Turkey breast
8. Summer squash
9. Cauliflower
10. Apples

Ten Favorite Miscellaneous Things

1. The desert
2. Hard training in an empty gym
3. Being at home
4. Mount Rainier
5. A thunderstorm, a fireplace and a good book
6. The stars (astronomy, not Hollywood)
7. A very good meal
8. Down comforters
9. Exploring an unknown place
10. Sleep

INDEX